FANS IN FASHION

Selections from
The Fine Arts Museums of San Francisco
by Anna G. Bennett,
with Ruth Berson

Published upon the occasion of an exhibition at
The Fine Arts Museums of San Francisco,
California Palace of the Legion of Honor, May 23-
August 30, 1981.

The exhibition and the catalogue have been supported by funds from Shreve & Company, The
Museum Society, and a group of private sponsors
and contributors.

ISBN 0-88401-037-6. Library of Congress
Catalogue Card No. 81-65612. All rights reserved.
No part of the contents of this book may be
reproduced without the written permission of the
publishers.

Front cover: *The Mask.* (cat. no. 10).
England, 1740-50. Gift of Susanne King Morrison
in memory of Elizabeth Brant King, 1980.66.

The Fine Arts Museums
of San Francisco
Charles E. Tuttle Co., Inc.
Rutland, Vermont and
Tokyo, Japan

TABLE OF CONTENTS

Corporate Sponsor
Shreve & Company

Sponsors and Contributors
Mrs. M.F. Allende
Mr. and Mrs. Ralph Bennett
Mrs. Gerald A. Bramwell
Mr. and Mrs. Willard Caro
Mr. and Mrs. Park Chamberlain
East Bay Fan Guild
Mr. and Mrs. Samuel B. Fortenbaugh, Jr.
Mrs. Grace R. Grayson
Mr. and Mrs. A. Adrian Gruhn
Ms. Jessie Jonas
Mrs. F.A. Jostes
Mr. and Mrs. John F. Merriam
Mr. and Mrs. Peter Morrison
Mrs. Louis Niggeman
Mrs. John Niven
Mrs. Ernst Ophuls
Mrs. Allan Starr
Mr. and Mrs. William Steen
Mr. Whitney Warren
Mrs. Osborne White

A museum basement storage occasionally produces a "sleeper," a cache of hidden treasures among its holdings. The rich and varied material of the textile department of The Fine Arts Museums of San Francisco has yielded more than one such surprise in recent years, resulting first in the publication of its majestic tapestries and now, at the other end of the telescope, its frivolous, fascinating fans.

The fans, along with costumes and other accessories, are among the Museums' oldest and least-known collections, formed by donation since 1895. Their fragility has discouraged exhibition. We make a rare exception to celebrate the publication of this catalogue by presenting seventy-six fans in context. The fans take center stage with a supporting cast of costumes and paintings. It is unlikely that these fans will be seen soon again in such array. This catalogue guarantees a kind of permanent access to the best of the collection.

Help came from without and within the Museums. The project was warmly supported by an international group of amateurs and professionals, many of them associated with the Victoria and Albert Museum, a focus of fan study. The catalogue of *Fans in Fashion* developed with their help; the exhibition was realized through the talent and devotion of a group of conservation assistants directed by our textile conservator, Birgitta Anderton.

The intellectual and motive force behind all this textile activity

— tapestries, costumes, and now fans — is Anna Bennett, curator extraordinary, who has always given generously of her time, often without recompense. Her mind like a fan oscillating at hummingbird speed, her curiosity darting to and fro in the neglected garden, she pauses just long enough to guide us to blooms we had overlooked till now. She has earned our respect and gratitude far beyond this season.

The collective efforts, however, would not have resulted in either a catalogue or an exhibition without the corporate sponsorship of Shreve & Company and generous gifts from a large group of sponsors and contributors. They have our warm thanks for furnishing this delight.

Ian McKibbin White
Director of Museums

The mounting interest in fans is confirmed by their conspicuous presence in antique shops and auctions and by the soaring prices they command. The nostalgic seventies brought fans back; the energy-conscious eighties may prolong their stay as guilt-free air conditioners, but the ultimate reason for their periodic revivals is the fan's inherent elegance and the human need for an expressive extension.

The reappearance of the fan urged the present publication of The Fine Arts Museums' collection. Our plan is to set the fans in context, stressing their role in daily life and showing them against silks and laces that echo the costumes of their day. Imagination on the part of the reader will do the rest, transporting them to the ballroom or the gazebo and restoring their restless motion.

Help with this effort came from colleagues, collectors, and specialists in other fields. In particular, Nancy Armstrong, well-known English lecturer in the Decorative Arts, provided advice and information at critical stages. Other officers and patrons of The Fan Circle — Helene Alexander, Madeleine Ginsburg, Avril Hart, and Felix Tal — assisted in various ways. The meager facts available for the entries were expanded by the informed opinions of Mrs. Armstrong, Ellen Dennis, Esther Oldham, Maria Rychlewska, and Edith Standen. The costume historian Dr. Douglas Russell helped with tricky dating. Specialists Robert Drewes, Barry Roth, and Jacqueline Schonewald of the California Academy of Sciences assisted with difficult identification of materials. Stephen Little of the Asian Art Museum illuminated the chinoiserie subjects. Sally Reichart clarified musical references,

and John Polt and Jean Lucelle assisted with translation. The experts did not always agree, but that is a problem with some historical precedence. Pliny, writing about the death of Cyrus the Great, said there were conflicting accounts of it and he had chosen the version he judged most likely to be true. In the same spirit, we have made arbitrary choices for which we accept responsibility.

The inertia of the early stages was overcome through the invaluable help of Sandra Lawrence who photographed, measured, and repaired the fans, infusing the project with the enthusiasm of a long-time collector. With the entries under way, we settled on a title, only to discover it had been used in 1975. We thank the organizers of *Fans in Fashion,* an exhibition held at Temple Newsam House, Leeds, and the Gallery of English Costume at Platt Hall, Manchester, and the author of the publication, Emmeline Leary, for endorsing our re-use of the title.

Ruth Berson's role has grown steadily as the work progressed. She is responsible for the notes amplifying the entries and for constructive suggestions throughout. A sensitive observer, gifted researcher, and loyal supporter, she has been an ideal collaborator. Two factors are responsible for the ultimate publication of the manuscript. The first is the determination of Ian McKibbin White, Director of The Fine Arts Museums, and Ann Heath Karlstrom, Publications Manager. The second is the generosity of a group of sponsors that lifted the project over a budgetary impasse and set it down safely at the printer's door.

Anna G. Bennett

The real business of fans is to attract attention, to move gracefully and charismatically through social events. Their season is brilliant but brief. Delicately constructed of perishable materials, fans grow more brittle and harder to handle with age. Many self-destruct; others come to rest in the twilight of museum storage, there to be laid on shallow trays like dried butterflies. Curators are reluctant to accelerate their deterioration by handling, with the result that fan exhibitions are rare. Many a fragile but intriguing collection, like that of The Fine Arts Museums, remains unknown and unsuspected by its own community. *Fans in Fashion* was undertaken to bring The Fine Arts Museums' fans a step nearer to the public by publishing a representative sample of the collection.

Choosing among the two hundred fans was not easy in the face of their astonishing variety. Gauze fans lay next to fans of thick buffalo hide. Sticks were made of sandalwood, tortoiseshell, ivory or mother-of-pearl. Some were severely plain, others painted, carved and encrusted with silver and gold. The shapes were equally unpredictable. One shaped like a racquet supported a stuffed warbler; another revolved by clockwork. Fashion's caprice was evident in the leaves, from the cool, sequined silks of Napoleon's First Empire to the cascading ostrich plumes of the 1920s. Such a bizarre mixture raised questions of provenance. Who did the collecting? By what route did the fans reach the Museums? Why fans at all in a cool and breezy climate?

A century ago San Francisco harbor was crowded with ships bringing merchandise of every kind to a rapidly growing city. Among the European art objects destined for the new mansions crowning the hills were antique fans for the drawing room vitrine and fans from Paris for the next reception. The importing fever produced private collections, and some of these moved into the public domain with the establishment of a city museum in 1895. Inspired by the Columbian Exposition of 1893 (see cat. no. 65), Michael H. de Young organized a fair for San Francisco in Golden Gate Park. The California Midwinter International Exposition of 1894-5 succeeded beyond expectations, leaving buildings, cash, and a few exhibits to start a city museum. This newly-formed Memorial Museum (soon to be renamed after Mr. de Young) inherited forty fans along with other material, and this number grew steadily by donation. Most of the charter donors gave the heavy-shouldered Spanish fans their hoop-skirted grandmothers had carried in the fifties and sixties, rather than the fans of their own day. Any account of the collection's beginning must include the names of those early donors Sarah Spooner, Mrs. Morton Mitchell and Archer M. Huntington.

"Damaged in the earthquake" was a recurrent entry in the registrar's records of 1906. The fans had suffered with other fragile items. The instinct for preservation, however, seemed to sharpen after the disaster, stimulating a new flood of random gifts. This pattern of giving produces broad representation, but rarely the sustained quality of a specialized collection.

The city acquired another museum in Lincoln Park, the gift of Mr. and Mrs. Adolph B. Spreckels in 1924. French in appearance and in inspiration, the new California Palace of the Legion of Honor attracted many French collections. None of them was better attuned to its setting than the French fans of the Warren family. The architect Whitney Warren is remembered professionally for his design of Grand Central Station and other vast public buildings in New York, but as a private collector he was attracted to beauty on a small scale. His important collection of eighteenth-century fans had been disbursed among his heirs. His son Whitney Warren, Jr., a trustee of the Legion of Honor, persuaded his sister, Mrs. Reginald Rives, and his niece, Mrs. Beatrice Greenough, to reunite the collection and present it to his museum.

The two city museums merged in 1972 as The Fine Arts Museums of San Francisco. All holdings were combined, a process that changed the scope and character of the collections. In the case of the fans, the result was remarkable. The variety of the de Young fans was complemented by examples of great quality from the Legion of Honor. Gifts from Osgood Hooker, Charlotte Elsasser, and in 1978 an extensive gift from Mrs. F.A. Jostes closed gaps in the representation. The unmistakable return of the fan to fashion in the 1980s assures a future of continuing growth and demands a re-examination and re-evaluation of the collection that has been formed by serendipity since 1895.

INTRODUCTION

Venus, the goddess of love, is often shown attempting to detain her lovers from the rougher sports of hunting and war. In Veronese's painting at the Prado she prolongs an enchanted moment in the garden by fanning Adonis as he sleeps, while Cupid holds a hunting dog in check. Venetian beauties of the sixteenth century carried just such flag-shaped fans as the one the artist placed in the hand of Venus. The fashion of fans spread from Italy to all the courts of Europe. The early flag-like forms and the jeweled court fans of ostrich plumes were succeeded by a fan that was infinitely more seductive. The folding fan from Asia, half-revealing, half-concealing, dominated fashion for three centuries. Light and maneuverable, it could project the mood of its owner. It pouted, sighed; it encouraged and rebuked. In Italy, as in China, the courtesans seem to have used it first, revealing again the guiding hand of Venus.

The romantic connection was a late development. The first fans must have been all function — palm leaves, perhaps, held by hands scarcely human. Ready-made "fans" grow obligingly in the tropics were they are needed most, and only a modest wit and an appositive thumb were required to put them to use. Fans played more serious roles when food gatherers became food producers. They separated chaff from wheat and kept hearths glowing. Winnowing fans and fire fans are still to be found in remote parts of the world, essentially unchanged from those painted in Egyptian tombs of the third millenium B.C.

Although working fans might be given a touch of color or design, their aesthetic development in general was unspectacular. On the other hand, the ceremonial fans of ancient Egypt commanded the greatest artistry, the richest materials. Their elegance of form and decoration complimented the majesty of their owners. Similar fans appear on Greek vases, with peacock feathers replacing ostrich plumes. The Greeks also used fans shaped like inverted hearts, a type common to Eastern countries. Did Phoenicians trading with Greece bring fans from both the South and the East along with their other wares?

Fans in Rome went by many names: the *muscarium* or fly-flap, the *vannus* or winnowing fan from which our word "fan" derives, the air-moving *flabellum*. Christianity incorporated the round *flabellum* into the ritual of the mass, using it to protect the Host from flies. According to Saint Jerome, the *flabellum* represented Chastity, which dispelled the flies that symbolized the Devil. The *flabellum* remained a cult object, confined to the sanctuary, until the twelfth century.

Thoroughly secular by the fourteenth century, fans multiplied in southern Europe, developing distinctive local forms in Italy. Catherine de Médicis is credited with bringing the fashion to France in 1549. Jeweled feather fans appear routinely in sixteenth-century portraits. The ostrich fan of Elizabeth's Armada portrait expresses ponderous majesty. Four years later the fan of the Ditchley portrait conveys a different message, manipulated by a queen who combined statecraft with coquetry. The folding fan from Asia had arrived.[1]

Paolo Veronese,
Venus and Adonis.
©Museo del Prado, Madrid.

By the time that Queen Elizabeth posed for her 1592 portrait holding an Asian-type fan, Portuguese and Spanish merchants were well established in the Far East and had supplied Europe for decades with porcelains, lacquers, and other orientalia. As early as 1565, Elizabeth was urged to enter the mercantile race for the riches of Cathay. She tried to correspond with the emperor of China, but her letters of 1596 and 1602 did not reach their destination. England's East India Company of 1599 and the Dutch East India Company formed three years later took over the trade previously monopolized by Portugal and Spain.[2]

Interacting factors fed the mania for China that engulfed Europe: the strange and unfamiliar beauty of imported objects and the pervasion of a dream. The Italians had much responsibility for the latter, beginning with Marco Polo's thirteenth-century account of Cathay's incredible riches and its just and gentle people. An annotated copy of Marco Polo's work accompanied Columbus on his voyage. Reports of Dutch travelers and merchants with something to gain fueled the legend, but the French, who had no luck with the mercantile adventure, contributed most to the fantasy. French Jesuit missionaries sketched the broad outlines of an idyllic land, and French taste and imagination supplied the details. The image of Cathay, developed in Europe, affected to some extent the export product. The Chinese were not averse to representing themselves as Europeans wished to see

them, thereby lessening the gap between "chinoiserie" art (originating in Europe) and objects made in Asia for export.

The balance of fact and fancy in chinoiserie art shifted from faithful imitation in the early years to free-wheeling invention in the mid-eighteenth century. In the East, sporadic "occidenterie" never advanced beyond the imitative stage. Emperor Ch'ien Lung ordered a summer palace in the French style, but no fantasy land developed comparable to the European kingdom of Cathay.[3]

The China theme in many European fans is confined to the sticks or altogether missing, but the basic debt to the East remains in the form of the fan itself. Certain types of folding fans had developed independently in Europe, but the dominant form, still in vogue, originated in ninth-century Japan and came to the West via China and Portuguese merchants in the sixteenth century.

The brisé fan, another Chinese export, retained more of its oriental character. The sticks (or blades) of brisé fans carry no separate leaf, but extend full length to provide a continuous surface for decoration. That surface was sometimes sandalwood, intricately carved, or ivory densely painted and covered with a fine varnish. Intense efforts had been made by western craftsmen to imitate the brilliant luster of Japanese lacquer. It could not be duplicated exactly, since the *Rhus vernicifera* tree producing the essential resin would not grow in Europe.[4] Other resins were substituted, made soluble in suitable ingredients and applied in layers to a richly decorated surface. This procedure, called "japanning," produced some remarkable effects, rivaling the oriental model. The decorative style of these early brisé fans was rich confusion, combining Chinese diaper patterns, flowers from Persian miniatures, Italian arabesques, and motifs from France. Reserved areas frequently contained blue-and-white porcelain scenes or small Chinese figures *en cartouche*.

M. Gheeraerts the Younger,
Queen Elizabeth I (detail).
National Portrait Gallery, London.

The desire for secrecy has brought into being many enigmatic languages in which thoughts are expressed by signs. None was more elegant than the fan language of the eighteenth and nineteenth centuries. It may have sprung spontaneously from the amorous intrigues of rococo society, but it used a system known to antiquity. It developed sometime between 1711 and 1740. In Addison's *Spectator* No. 102 of 1711, fans are not communicators but deadly weapons, the use of which must be taught in an academy of pseudo-martial arts. By 1740, however, fans talked, as noted by *The Gentleman's Magazine*. Fan users had begun to spell out words by the significant positions of their fans.

The alphabet can be divided neatly into five groups of five letters each by omitting the letter "J": a-e, f-k, l-p, q-u, v-z. Any letter can be designated by a two-number combination, the first indicating the group, the second the position of the letter within its group. Thus "l" can be expressed as 3:1, that is, the first letter in the third group. All that was needed to adapt the ancient system to fans was to agree that numbers 1 through 5 would be represented by moving the fan to certain agreed-upon positions:

Number 1: The fan in the left hand moves to the right arm.
Number 2: The fan in the right hand moves to the left arm.
Number 3: The fan is placed against the heart.
Number 4: The fan is raised to the lips.
Number 5: The fan touches the brow.

Thus, the word "l-o-v-e" could be signaled by eight fan signs: 3:1, 3:4, 5:1, 1:5, a precise but time-consuming system.

After two and half centuries it is difficult to gauge the extent to which fans were actually used for communication. Certainly fan makers recognized the commercial advantage of fan language and promoted it by publishing a special type of fan called the "Conversation Fan." Charles Francis Badini's Fanology fan, published in 1797 by the fan maker William Cock, has the directions for fan spelling engraved on the leaf as an aid to memory.

The word-spelling method was slow. Another, faster fan language emerged in which entire words or phrases could be expressed by a single movement of the fan. The development of two distinct systems for communicating with fans has its parallel in the two systems used by the deaf who talk with their hands. They can spell out words by shaping the letters with their fingers or they can express the entire word or phrase by a single gesture of the hand. Fingerspelling and signing can be mixed in manual communication, but the two fan-language systems are mutually exclusive.

The faster method apparently originated in Spain where particularly severe social strictures encouraged its development. The tract was translated from the Spanish of its inventor, Fenella, into German by Frau Bartholomeus. The Parisian fan maker Pierre Duvelleroy published a shortened form in English. Duvelleroy's interests, commercially inspired, dovetailed with those of a society

that officially endorsed propriety and privately winked at intrigue.
Examples taken from Deuvelleroy's printed list are revealing:

Twirling the fan in the left hand: *We are watched.*

Carrying the fan in the right hand before the face: *Follow me.*

Covering the left ear with the open fan: *Do not betray our secret.*[5]
The fans used to sign or spell out messages were held by women.
A special kind of conversation fan was designed to be shared in
close quarters by a mixed couple. The left side of the fan is
printed with thirty numbered questions to ask a woman. The
right side has thirty possible replies. Sample questions are paired
with random answers:

Q (no. 19): Etes-vous capricieuse? *(Are you fickle?)*

A (no. 7): C'est mon faible. *(That's my weakness)*

Q (no. 7): Etes-vous facile à séduire? *(Are you easy to seduce?)*

A (no. 24): La question est indiscrète. *(The question is indiscreet.)*
Further entertainment in the form of picture puzzles is provided by
the guard sticks.[6]

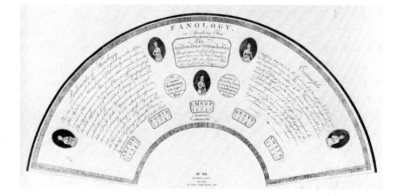

Above: Fanology Fan, from Lady Schreiber's collec-
tion. Reproduced by courtesy of the Trustees of the
British Museum.
Below: Conversation Fan. Felix Tal collection,
Amsterdam.

Centuries of westernization failed to remove altogether the sense that the fan was a foreign novelty not to be taken quite seriously. While many Chinese and Japanese fan leaves bear famous signatures, a European leaf signed "Watteau" or "Boucher" arouses immediate suspicion. We do not expect to find fan leaves painted by major artists. The East-West contrast extends to the sticks. Oriental sticks seem to avoid any decoration that might intrude on the subtleties of the leaf. European sticks, heavily loaded with ornament, compete openly and successfully for attention. Fans of the West, if not Art, are art objects of remarkable parts.

From the beginning, guild regulations forbade a master fan maker to produce his own sticks. He must purchase them from a comb maker, a goldsmith, or a dealer in fancy goods of horn, wood, or shell, depending on his choice of material.[7] The gilding was the work of another separate group unlikely to use restraint. Fifteen to twenty workers handled a fan from the gluing of the leaf to the setting of the rivet. Each craftsman's skill contributed to the fan's multifaceted decoration.

The Leaf. Before work on the leaf could begin, the material for it had to be prepared elsewhere. Vellum was an early choice.[8] Indeed, leather-gilders formed part of the group to whom Louis XIV granted a charter. The delicate skin of a young (preferably unborn) lamb, kid, or calf was made smooth and pliant by liming, scraping, stretching, and treating with chalk and pumice. In the seventeenth

century the vellum was decorated by cutting out patterns with tiny knives so that the leaf resembled *reticella* lace. Later vellum leaves were painted, usually with gouache. Many of these survive today, but the material most frequently encountered is paper. Until the 1790s, paper was made by hand, much of it at l'Anglée, the great factory south of Paris described by Diderot. He recorded every step of the process by which rags were converted into paper.

Two paper sections were glued together for each leaf, then dried and trimmed to prepare them for the painter (Diderot, Pls. I and II). Men as well as women painted the leaves. Fan designs follow a discernible course of development. Earlier images are placed squarely across the width of the fan without reference to the shape of the leaf, in the manner of easel paintings. Later designs accommodate somewhat to the curve, with the figures tending to slip into central and lateral groupings. By the third quarter of the eighteenth century, these groups are often framed in cartouches as medallions and set off by a plain background. (Fan painting and porcelain painting are not far apart; when the Sèvres factory experienced a shortage of porcelain painters, fan painters were called to fill the gap.) The painting finished, thin gold paint was brushed delicately and selectively onto the gouache to give the leaf a final touch of luxury.

The Sticks. Since the sticks were made of more durable material than that of the leaf, they often outlasted it. Worn-out or damaged leaves could be replaced, with the result that the sticks of surviving fans are sometimes found to be older than their leaves. The sticks are the fan's skeleton, providing its strength and mobility. They are held at the base by a rivet that is often set with a brilliant stone. From the top of the sticks, narrow extensions known as *ribs* pass behind a single leaf or between the two sides of a double leaf. Full-length end sticks, called *guards*, protect both leaf and inner sticks.

Ivory and mother-of-pearl, both exotic materials from distant lands, were favorite choices for sticks. Tortoiseshell and metal were used less frequently. Bone made an inexpensive substitute for ivory and horn for tortoiseshell.[9] Imported raw materials were worked in European ateliers, but traders also supplied ready-made sticks from the Orient.

Mother-of-pearl, taken from the iridescent lining of certain pearl oyster shells, made spectacular sticks. Shells in general exerted a powerful fascination over the eighteenth century. Villas added shell-covered grottoes; marquetry furniture gleamed with pearly inlay. The form of the shell itself became the dominant motive of the rococo style. The shells were converted into delicate sticks by means of small saws, files, and dilute sulfuric acid. Lamination was necessary to achieve the length needed for the guards. The work passed successively through the hands of the sawyer, grinder, straightener, cutter, shaper, and engraver. Gold and silver leaf was applied to the mother-of-pearl in the form of figural scenes, often

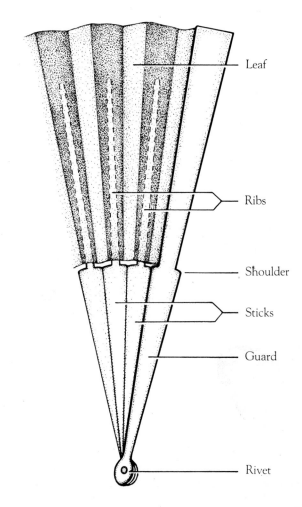

Leaf

Ribs

Shoulder

Sticks

Guard

Rivet

13

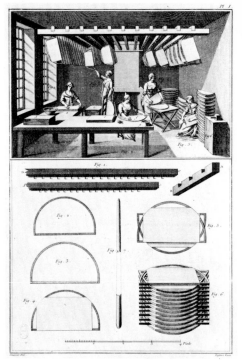

Pl. I

backed by very thin sheets of especially brilliant mother-of-pearl. In France the province of l'Oise was famous for its mother-of-pearl work.

If mother-of-pearl reminded the eighteenth century of the beauty of the shell, ivory conjured up for them the mystery of the Orient. The tusks of the male elephant were the main source of commercial ivory. Europeans drew their supply mainly from Africa; the Chinese preferred the softer and whiter ivory of India and Ceylon.

From the time of Francis I, Dieppe was an ivory-carving center. Until mechanical carving was introduced in the nineteenth century,[10] the carvers of Dieppe, like those of Canton, used the saw, gouge, and mallet, the rasp, file, chisel, and scraper. Deep undercutting and a high degree of technical skill characterizes the work done in China, but the long-cherished notion that Chinese carvers worked with the ivory submerged in water has recently been questioned.[11]

Final Steps. The later stages of assembling the fan were greatly simplified in 1760 by the invention of the pleating mould.[12] Diderot's Pl. III, dating from 1765, shows two moulds made for fans of differing proportions and a mould being used in the factory (Diderot, Pl. III, Figs. 2, 3 and Fig. 1 above, left side). The fan is placed on the wooden mould with care to balance the design and to avoid having essential details fall in the pleats. Pleating lines are then made on the fan by pressing the leaf into the radial scoring of the mould with the small instrument shown in Fig. 7. When the scoring is complete, the leaf is removed and a half-circle cut out for the sticks. The leaf is pleated by folding at every scored line, then pinching a pleat between each fold, as shown in Pl. IV. A fan leaf that has reached this point is ready for its sticks. A passage must be made for each rib by pushing a probe between the glued layers of the leaf (Diderot, Pl. III, Fig 1 above, right). This done, the sticks can be united with the leaf by threading the ribs into the prepared passages as shown in Pl. IV, Fig. 14. The upper edge is bound if desired, and the assemblage of parts is complete.[13]

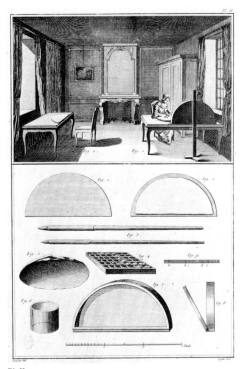

Pl. II

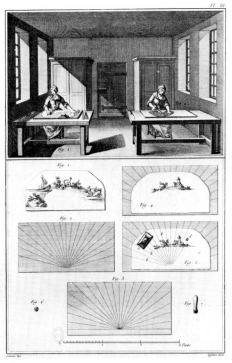

Pl. III

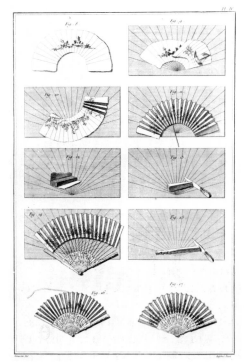

Pl. IV

Pls. I-IV, Diderot, *Encyclopédie: Eventailliste*.
Photo: Bibliothèque Nationale, Paris.

Notes to the Introduction

Abbreviated references cite the authors name, year of publication where necessary, and page or chapter number. The full titles appear at the end of the Catalogue in the List of Works Consulted.

1. *The Hand of Venus*
   The early history of the fan and its role in different cultures has been told and retold since Blondel's long account of 1875 (Ch. 1-7). With each retelling, certain details disappear and others are added. Rhead in 1910 (Ch. 1-5) and Green in 1973 (Ch. 1-3) cover much the same ground, and Armstrong summarized it twice, in 1974 and 1978.

2. *The Celestial Vision*
   Anthony Jenckyson's letter of 1565 begged Elizabeth to encourage "this famous discovery of Cathay of great renown" (Belevitch-Stankevitch, Intro., p. xxvii).

3. Bowie, Fig. 179 and p. 106. Also, see no. 11 of this catalogue.

4. Stalker and Parker's sixteenth-century account of japanning makes an interesting comparison with the complete modern study by Hans Huth.

5. *Cryptic Communicators*
   Bertha de Vere Green's very full treatment of fan signing (pp. 154-61) follows Rhead in tracing the development of the system from the Spanish to the English version (Rhead, pp. 136-37) and combines it with Rhead's explanation of fan spelling (Rhead, p. 253). For a shorter summary, see Armstrong, 1974, pp. 182-3.

6. Felix Tal's two-way talking fan was exhibited at Beeckestijn, Netherlands, in 1979. It has two picture puzzles on its guards. On the right guard appear a wooden shoe (or *sabeau*) + T (pronounced *té*) + m'e + a cask (or *tonne*). Reformed, the words and letters spell *Sa beauté m'étonne* (His/her beauty astounds me). On the left guard we see an L (prounced *elle*) + *est* + 100 (*cent*, or its homonym *sans*) + a die (or *dé*) + a scythe (*faux*, or its homonym *faut*). Reformed, these produce the sentence *Elle est sans défaut* (She is without fault). This explanation was kindly supplied by J.G. Berkhout at the generous suggestion of Felix Tal.

7. *Assemblage of Parts*
   For guild regulations, see Blondel, pp. 81-2.

8. Throughout the catalogue, the word *vellum* is used in its broadest sense: "a fine-grained unsplit lambskin, kidskin, or calfskin" (*Webster's New Collegiate Dictionary*).

9. Tortoiseshell as a stick material has not been included in this discussion because it appears rarely in The Fine Arts Museums' collection. The hawksbill turtle (*Eretmochelys imbricata*) is the sole source of commercial tortoiseshell (Cousteau, Appendix IV). Darcet discovered a way to imitate by using muriatic acid on bone (Blondel, pp. 212-13). True shell is lighter in weight. Later methods of simulating tortoiseshell made use of pressed resins.

10. Alphonse Baude's invention of mechanical carving in 1859 changed the quality and value of fans (Blondel, p. 197).

11. Crossman questions this long-held belief on the basis of contemporary observations (Crossman, p. 208, refers to Osmond Tiffany's *The Canton Chinese*, Boston and Cambridge, 1849, P. 75).

12. See Rhead, p. 121.

13. M. Gostelow summarizes the assembly process at some length, using the Diderot plates as illustrations (Gostelow, pp. 18-21).

FANS: 1700-1800

Fashion determined the volume of the fan industry as well as the size of the product. Fans of majestic proportions (*à grand vol*) balanced skirts held out by paniers. They dwindled to "imperceptibles" to match the deflated skirts of Revolutionary times. To carry a fan of *grand luxe* became unfashionable as well as politically unwise. Leaf painters and stick gilders found themselves idle as the industry faltered. Women did not, however, lay their fans aside. Charlotte Corday, for example, called on Marat with a dagger in one hand and a fan in the other. That fan was probably in the pared-down mode of the moment, possibly printed with a political message. The temporary collapse of the fan industry was unlamented by the world at large, including the brothers de Goncourt, writing a little later. They noted the abrupt halt of a "commerce of the superfluous, the useless, of fantasy, nothingness, eye recreation, diversion for jaded senses." The object of their moral indignation was actually not the industry, but the society it supplied and mirrored so faithfully.

There was a fan for every social occasion. Those that went to church properly showed bible subjects like Rebekah and the twins (no.9), Jacob and Rachel (no.14) or Ruth and Boaz (no.13), an exemplar of Virtue Rewarded. Others were intended for weddings and generally depict lovers burning their rose crowns on the altar of Hymen (nos.2,24,25). Fans assisted the absent-minded to remember the dates of holidays (no.21 shows the feast days of 1773) or served as maps (no.28, "The Ladies Travelling Fann of England and Wales"). Fans in shades of gray supplied the mourner

(no.18). Others, smartly journalistic, recorded current events (no.26, the *Balloon Ascension*). The fan held up before society mirrored it sensitively. We share a summer afternoon with those playing battledore and shuttlecock or bowling on the green (no.3), or stand behind a fence with the peasant woman who spies on the antics of the local country gentry (no.6).

Even more intriguing, because possibly more significant, are those fans that lead us away from daily life toward the great escape routes of the eighteenth century. The dream of Arcadia came first, born of the pastoral romances of the seventeenth century. Elegant Chloes neglect their sheep to listen to their shepherds (nos.8,15, 20). Fabulous Cathay was no further away than Arcadia, attained at times by a quick flip of the fan (nos.8,9, and 11, reverses). There agrarian simplicity blended effortlessly with refined sensibility. Arcadia and Cathay, however, paled as the sun of Antiquity rose higher in the sky and gentle sages and beribboned shepherdesses were trampled by an Olympian stampede. Diana and her maidens swarmed through the woods (no.16), Bacchus roamed the shore (no.11). Helen and Europa were abducted (nos.1,17) and Iphigenia had a close call (no.4). Human endeavors were personified by winged amorini (no.31), and all the gods and goddesses of Olympus swooped down to dignify human events (no.2). But the Olympians did not succeed in destroying the competition completely. A shepherd in modern dress plays a forlorn little tune as he wanders into the nineteenth century (no.30).

THE ABDUCTION OF HELEN

France or Netherlands, 1700-25

Italy, 1715-25

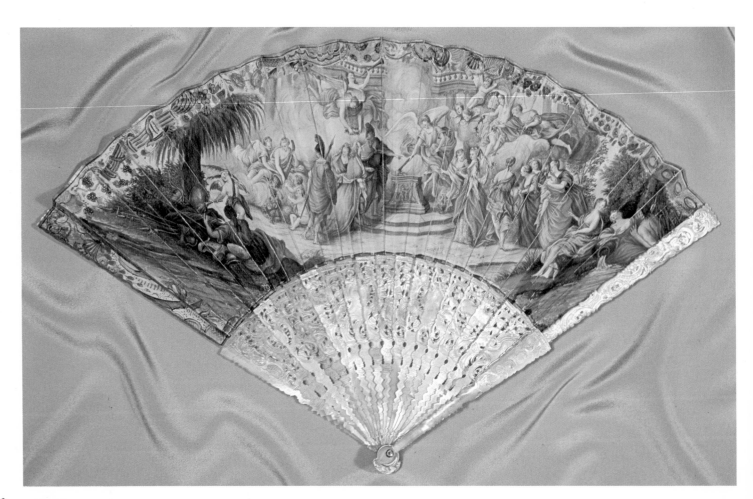

France, 1730-35

Netherlands, 1740-45

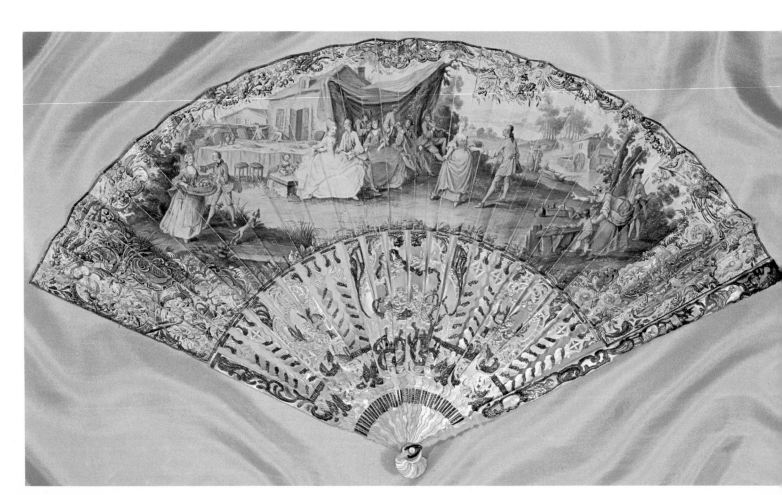

France or Netherlands, 1747-50

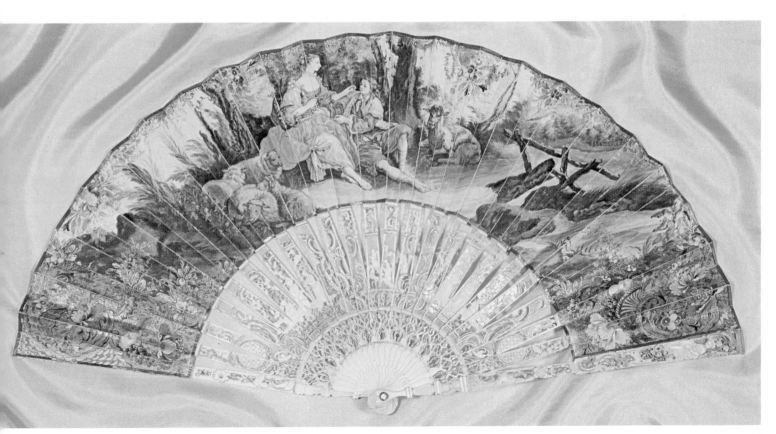

Netherlands, ca. 1760

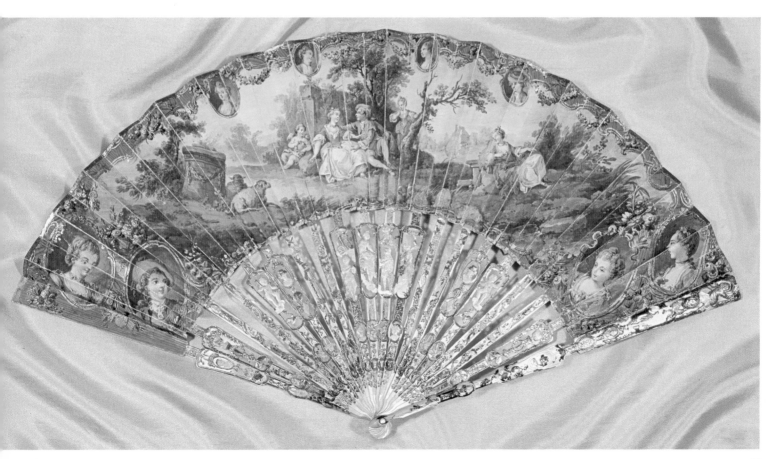

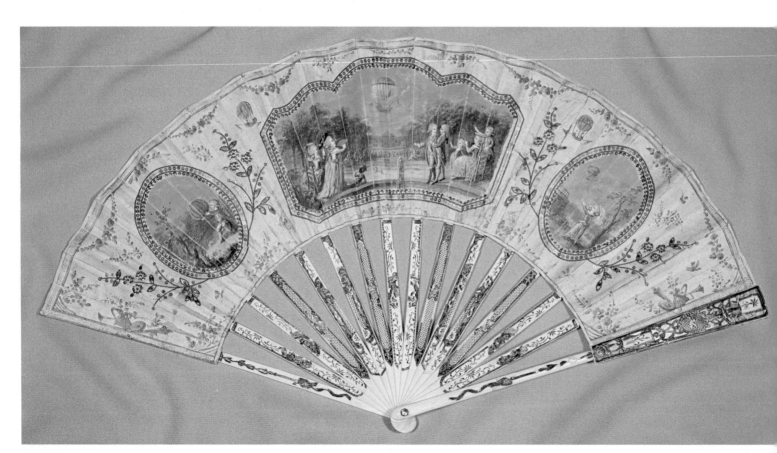

The event that precipitated the Trojan War is shown as a violent abduction. Helen's arm is raised in a gesture of protest like that of the Sabine women, but the jewels she takes along suggest premeditation. An inset pearl frame sets off the scene from a dense background of ornament including four chinoiserie figures.

On the reverse, another surprise encounter takes place in contemporary dress. The painting is unremarkable, but the craftsmanship sets this early brisé fan in a class apart. The guard stick is protected by a mother-of-pearl thumb guard and decorated with a paste inset at the rivet.

France or Netherlands, first quarter 18th century
Oil paint on ivory, varnished
Guard: 21 cm (8¼ in)
Gift of Archer M. Huntington
Acc. no. 16,261

Brides often gave their attendants fans with wedding themes as mementos, and grooms commissioned elaborate fans for their fiancées. This Regency fan depicts a noble couple before the altar of Hymen with gods and goddesses arriving by land, sea, and air.

Cupid (left) puts a torch to the weapons of Mars. Fruit and flowers pour from the cornucopia of Abundance. River gods (right) watch as Hymen lights the sacred fire. The flowing wig and robe worn by the groom at center support an early date.

Italy, 1715-25
Gouache on vellum (front), paper (back)
Mother-of-pearl sticks; guard: 28cm (11in)
Gift of Mrs. Reginald Rives
Acc. no. 1978.10.5

Summer in full swing is enjoyed in a country garden. Flowers are tended at left, games played at right, including bowling on the green and battledore and shuttlecock. The parasol, straw hats and fan tell of the heat of the day. The loose contouche of the lady at left has fallen back to reveal her stays.

Like adults, small girls wear paniers supporting large skirts. Hair is powdered. On the reverse, two women play with rabbits, a youth presents flowers. Two illegible signatures appear beside the figures. Gold-leaf couples with tubs of grapes are enclosed in rocaille frames of silver on the mother-of-pearl sticks.

France, 1730-35
Gouache on vellum (front), paper (back)
Mother-of-pearl sticks; guard: 29 cm (11½ in)
Gift of Mrs. B. Greenough
Acc. no. 1964.97

The Greeks waiting at Aulis for a favorable wind to take them to Troy were told to sacrifice Iphigenia. According to Aeschylus, she died, but Euripides gave the story another ending. As the knife was raised for the blow, the goddess Artemis appeared, carried off the maiden, and left a deer in her place.

The landscape on the reverse shows a bridge over a river and old buildings bathed in golden light. The tapering mother-of-pearl sticks are painted, gilded, and backed with iridescent mother-of-pearl. Cartouches enclose courting couples and pastoral motifs in gold leaf. The rivet is inset with paste.

Italy, ca. 1730
Gouache on vellum with varnish
Mother-of-pearl sticks; guard: 29 cm (11½ in)
Gift of Mrs. Reginald Rives
Acc. no. 1978.10.19

Five people inhabit a very small island. The central trio, dressed for the Italian Comedy, hold shepherds' houlettes but have dispensed with sheep. Their practical companions wash clothes and fish at the water's edge.

At either edge of the scene a musical trophy on a gold ground is bordered by peacock feathers. The leaf has been shortened and remounted on sticks of a later date (ca. 1765). Gold and mother-of-pearl have been applied to the sticks that are painted blue, red, and green.

Italy, 1730-40 (leaf)
Gouache on paper
Ivory sticks; guard: 26cm (10¼ in)
Gift of Mrs. B. Greenough
Acc. no. 1964.89

A wedding is celebrated by the rural gentry. Fiddles and a hurdy-gurdy provide music for dancing as the wedding feast is laid out. At right a peasant mother leans over the fence to point out the bride to her son.

A Netherlandish origin would explain the combination of convincing rusticity and exotic details. Squirrels and fantastic birds inhabit the surrounding decoration. The gold rocaille is enriched with fruits and flowers. Encrusted spiral columns heighten the rich effect.

Netherlands, 1740-45
Gouache on vellum (front), paper (back)
Mother-of-pearl sticks; guard: 26.7 cm (10½ in)
Gift of Mrs. B. Greenough
Acc. no. 1964.87

this scene thinly painted in gouache, a village
...auty wearing wide paniers is the center of a
...spute. The leather-clad rustic on her left is
...uarely in the tradition of David Teniers. The
...verse shows a round tower and a row of
...osses.

A shepherd musician appears on the guard
against a background of beige silk. The sticks are
pierced and carved. Ribbon-like borders of
mother-of-pearl enclose three cartouches of hunting symbols, sheep, and two women, one swing-
ing and the other fanning.

Netherlands, 1740-50
Gouache on vellum (front), paper (back)
Ivory sticks; guard: 26cm (10¼ in)
Gift of Sarah Spooner
Acc. no. 25500

A beribboned shepherdess offers her lover a grape in a pastoral idyll after François Boucher. The faces differ from the original, suggesting an attempt at portraiture, perhaps for a wedding. The leaf, almost opening to a full half-circle, is held by exquisitely carved, pearl-backed sticks.

The reverse shows a familiarity with Chinese painting. A bearded scholar, attendant, and friend enjoy a garden of giant peonies with a grotesque rock like those from T'ai-hu (The Great Lake) that were a common feature of Chinese gardens.

France or Netherlands, 1747-50
Gouache on paper, with vellum repairs
Ivory sticks; guard: 26 cm (10¼ in)
Gift of Mrs. B. Greenough
Acc. no. 1964.91

A majestic leaf, opening a full 180°, is held by pierced ivory sticks encrusted with powdered mother-of-pearl. The two children, shown with their mother in an interior, appear again on either side, one with dogs and hunting gear and the other with gardening tools — perhaps representing Rebekah, Esau, and Jacob.

Many church fans with biblical subjects were made in the Netherlands. A Dutch attribution is supported by the reverse side with its faithful imitation of Chinese painting. Tea is served to a scholar by an attendant in a rocky garden with large-scale peonies. At right a man points to a monkey in a tree.

Netherlands, ca. 1760
Gouache on vellum
Ivory sticks; guard: 30 cm (11¾ in)
Gift of Sarah Spooner
Acc. no. 25494

Every fan has the potential for concealment. In the case of the mask fan, the mystery is heightened by cut-out eyes through which one can spy, undetected. Six similar fans are known in public and private collections. All have the central ovoid mask, but the side scenes differ, some being distinctly Spanish in flavor.

All appears English here. Three of the four scenes are set in the open countryside. Two couples picnic and hold hands while, above, two ladies and a man on a quiet river punt past a distant spire. The townscape at left showing a lady carried in a sedan chair appears as well on a fan now at the Kremlin.

England, 1740-50
Gouache on vellum
Ivory sticks; guard: 28 cm (11 in)
Gift of Susanne King Morrison
in memory of Elizabeth Brant King
Acc. no. 1980.66

Ariadne, abandoned by Theseus on the island of Naxos, was discovered by Bacchus as she slept on the shore. Several copies of Guido Reni's famous lost painting of the subject have survived. An unmounted fan leaf at the Victoria and Albert Museum shows the same figures in a wooded grove.

On the reverse, a bearded potentate receives visitors in a curious audience hall where violins play in the background. Such an eclectic mixture of Chinese, Persian, and western elements might appear merely fantasy had not Emperor Ch'ien Lung built a European-style palace north of the Forbidden City.

Italy, 1750-60
Gouache on vellum
Horn sticks; guard: 27.3 cm (10¾ in)
Gift of Mrs. B. Greenough
Acc. no. 1964.102

The face of the fan shows peasants dancing to the music of tambourine and fiddle. Holes left in the guards probably once held precious stones. Fans of this kind were brought home as souvenirs by eighteenth-century travelers making the grand tour.

The reverse has a scene of the harbor at Naples with the lighthouse at the end of the Molo Grande that often appears in views of Vesuvius. The lighthouse, built in the fifteenth century, was still a landmark in the eighteenth.

Italy, ca. 1750
Gouache on vellum
Mother-of-pearl sticks; guard: 31 cm (12¼ in)
Gift of Mrs. B. Greenough
Acc. no. 1964.90

The story of Ruth's devotion to her dead husband's mother made an attractive example of Virtue Rewarded, suitable for a church fan. Boaz is shown inviting Ruth to glean with the maidens of his household. The rich floral border, well-painted oxen, and large-scale plant in the foreground are Netherlandish touches.

On the reverse, Ruth kneels with a sheaf of wheat. The sticks are carved rather flatly with Italian Comedy figures and birds flanking a central cartouche. Carved figures on the guards are set off by a backing of iridescent mauve foil. A paste is inset at the rivet.

Netherlands, 1740-50
Gouache on vellum
Ivory sticks; guard: 29 cm (11½ in)
Gift of Mrs. B. Greenough
Acc. no. 1964.98

Jacob rolled the stone from the well so that his cousin Rachel could water her father's flock. The strange rendering of this Old Testament story probably represents an oriental artist's unfamiliarity with western faces, western foliage, and with the source of the incident itself.

The leaf was originally wider. The damage sustained at the right edge necessitated a shortening of the leaf and its remounting on new sticks. These are crudely pierced and painted. A thin backing of mother-of-pearl survives in places. The sticks may date from the nineteenth century.

China export (to Netherlands), 1750-75
Gouache on paper
Ivory sticks; guard: 29 cm (11½ in)
Gift of Mrs. Reginald Rives
Acc. no. 1978.10.1

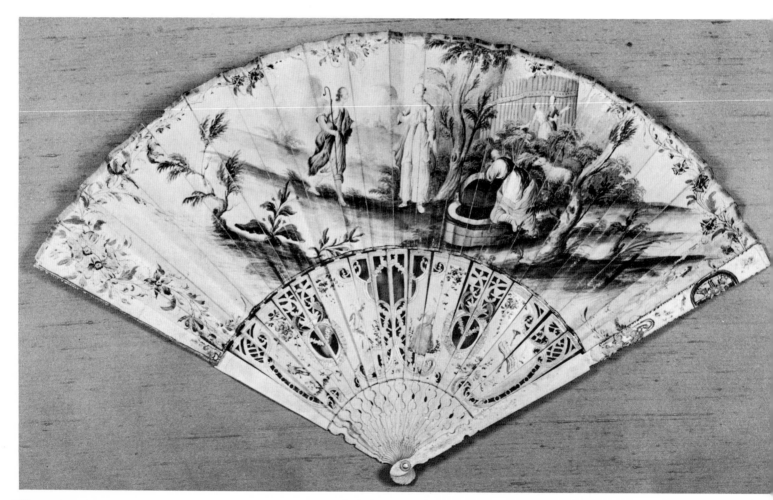

The declaration of love made in a rural setting is greeted with varying degrees of interest and surprise. Cupid, ready with his rose crown, awaits the outcome as fire burns on the altar of Hymen. The fan was probably commissioned for a wedding. The portraits linked at lower left may represent the engaged couple.

The medallions flanking the scene and the four small ovals across the top demonstrate the mid-century vogue for miniature portraits. The theme is repeated at several levels on the exquisite sticks and guards. The other individuals pictured on the leaf may be members of the wedding party.

France, 1755-60
Gouache on vellum (front), paper (back)
Mother-of-pearl sticks; guard: 26.7 cm (10½ in)
Gift of Mrs. Robert Homans
Acc. no. 1979.59.8

No accommodation was made for the curve of the fan in this painting of Diana relaxing with her entourage. The scene, covering the entire leaf, was cut to fit long, narrow sticks with some foreground losses. Minerva in battle dress decorates the reverse, retouched after the mounting.

The fine ungilded sticks have medallions in tiers, some with delicate piercing and chinoiserie figures, others with grill patterns from Chinese garden screens. The rivet is provided with a mother-of-pearl washer.

Netherlands or Germany, 1740-50
Gouache on paper
Ivory sticks; guard: 28.5 cm (11¼ in)
Gift of Mr. and Mrs. Floyd F. Reighley
Acc. no. 1956.82

A simplified but faithful copy of François Boucher's painting of 1747 occupies the central position, framed by smaller scenes that interlock like jig-saw pieces. There are dancers and two views of Venice, with a band of chinoiserie across the throat. The predominating colors are cool blue-green and warm Chinese red.

The reverse shows romantic ruins, Italianate landscapes, and blue and white porcelain designs. A miniature portrait appears on each convex guard. The fan may have been intended for a wedding or as a souvenir of Venice where lacquer working reached a high level of skill.

France or Italy, ca. 1750
Oil paint on ivory, varnished
Guard 21 cm (8¼ in)
Gift of Archer M. Huntington
Acc. no. 16,242

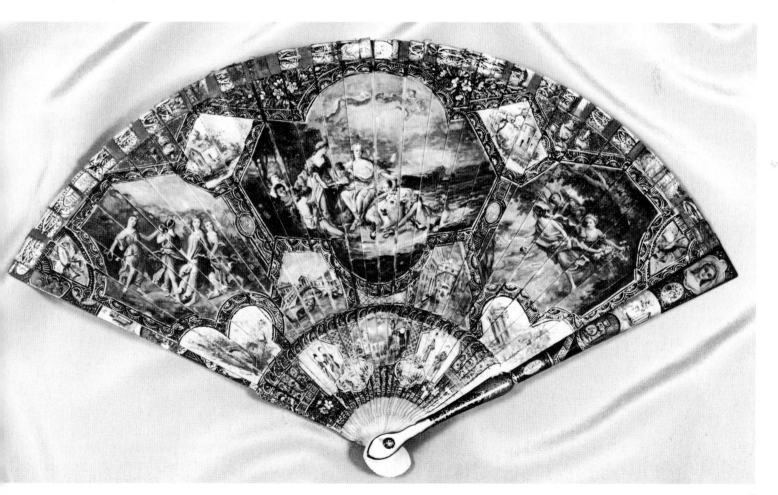

The absence of color identifies this as a mourner's fan. The monument itself is not conclusive, for many monuments served as backdrops for scenes of gallantry, enforcing the *tempus fugit* theme. Here the "shepherd" is departing, and the gate and crosses (reverse) confirm the idea of loss and separation.

Division of the pictorial area into three cartouches points to the second half of the eighteenth century. The plain sticks and general restraint suggest an English provenance. An elegiac note is struck by the quiet sheep and the swan swimming before a bridge that seems to have been bent to accommodate it.

England, 1760-70
Ink and wash on paper
Ivory sticks; guard: 26.7 cm (10½ in)
Gift of Mrs. Reginald Rives
Acc. no. 1978.10.4

The deep blue background suggests a German origin. Doll-like dancers in Italian Comedy costumes pirouette and scatter flowers to the music of a musette. The central scene and the two lateral ones of irregular shape are linked by pink and blue ribbons meandering over the surface and by flowers strewn at random.

The guards and twenty-four narrow mother-of-pearl sticks are encrusted with gold and silver leaf, forming three cartouches. These correspond in size and number to the scenes of the leaf. The growing interest in classicism is demonstrated by the dancing gold-leaf figures on the sticks.

Germany, ca. 1760
Gouache on paper
Mother-of-pearl sticks; guard: 28cm (11 in)
Gift of Mrs. Reginald Rives
Acc. no. 1978.10.3

Elegant couples in a misty landscape recall the fêtes galantes of the early eighteenth century, but some of the magic is missing. Here the musette, houlette, and songbook have been put aside and attention is focused on a tethered bird. The soaring coiffures of the ladies place the scene in the 1770s.

The guards carry a double portrait of a young couple. On the sticks putti hold gold-leaf medallion portraits, possibly representing Louis XVI and Marie Antoinette. On the center sticks a woman receives a floral crown while Cupid aims an arrow. Thin rods of green glass are inset on the sticks.

France, 1770-75
Gouache on vellum (front), paper (back)
Mother-of-pearl sticks; guard: 26.7 cm (10½ in)
Gift of Dr. Catherine Pike
Acc. no. 78.72.1

Easter holds the central spot on the leaf of this aid-to-memory fan that lists the important holy days of 1773. Four tapering panels, similar in shape to the top of the guard, enclose the days to celebrate joyously and those to be observed with self-restraint.

Four standing figures in the intermediate spaces personify the seasons. Small circles above their heads give the names of the months, the number of days in each, and their zodiacal signs. Other aid-to-memory fans provide maps, almanacs, dance steps, words and music, and the rules for social games, like the Fanology fan on page 11.

France, 1773
Gouache on paper
Ivory sticks; guard: 27.3 cm (10¾ in)
California Midwinter International Exposition
Acc. no. 3829

Brightly colored "domino" papers, stenciled or block-printed with bold, simple designs, lined chests, drawers, and books or served as wallpaper and fan leaves. A society in search of simplicity was charmed by the wallpaper fan's fresh informality, an effect heightened by slapdash workmanship.

The carelessly applied tan ground is organized by paired bamboo-like verticals and wavy lines with pink and blue roses filling the intervening spaces. An oval sketch of lovers under a bright blue sky occupies the central position. Crudely pierced bone sticks have flower-like touches of color.

France, late 18th century
Gouache on paper
Bone sticks; guard: 26cm (10¼in)
California Midwinter International Exposition
Acc.no.3809

A "Chinese" smoker with a long, thin pipe rests on a chair of European inspiration. His features recall portraits of the Chinese Emperor K'ang Hsi. Flowers were added at the sides when the printed image was colored by hand.

By the end of Louis XV's reign, printed fans and eastern imports became numerous. The plain ivory sticks express a trend toward this greater simplicity. The delicate flowering branches resemble some of the painted taffetas of the period in their graceful placement.

France, 1770-80
Hand-colored print on paper
Ivory sticks; guard: 25.4cm (10in)
Gift of Mrs. Robert Homans
Acc. no. 1979.59.6

Two lovers sacrifice their rose crowns on the altar of the god Hymen who presides over all marriages. Gold thread applied in chain stitch and multicolored sequins cover the leaf with garlands and floral sprays. A circle with two flaming hearts surmounts each lateral cartouche.

The narrow, widely-spaced ivory sticks are carved and encrusted with silver and gold leaf. The central six form a design of man, woman, and boy surrounded by colored foil dots. Black and blue jay feathers, once heavily applied, survive in some areas. Both sticks and leaf show compulsive horror vacui.

Germany, ca. 1780
Gouache on silk, gold thread and sequins
Ivory sticks; guard: 27.3 cm (10¾ in)
Gift of Mrs. Reginald Rives
Acc. no. 1978.10.2

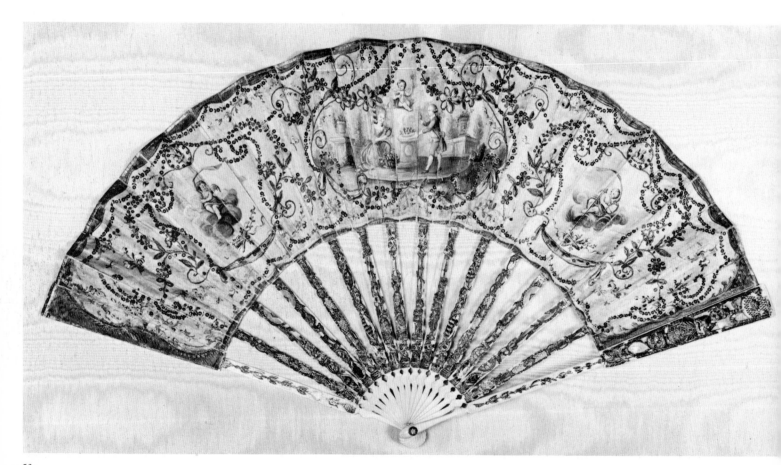

Hymen, holding a blazing torch, has led the wedding procession into a vaulted temple. As the lovers approach the altar, the goddess Aphrodite hands down a floral crown. In the lateral extensions, the imposing presence of Abundance (right) and Prudence (left) seem to augur well for the future.

The fan offers a striking comparison with its predecessor (no. 24). Classical restraint and straight lines invest the theme with new dignity. The three-part division is observed but handled in a way that suggests a continuous space. The fan is remarkable for its design, fine detail, and impeccable taste.

Italy(?), 1780-85
Watercolor on paper
Mother-of-pearl sticks; guard: 28 cm (11 in)
Gift of Mrs. Reginald Rives
Acc. no. 1978.10.13

Balloon fever was epidemic in the early 1780s. Spectators in the fan's central scene watch a balloon carry MM. Charles and Robert high above the Tuileries on December 1, 1783. The balloon theme is repeated in the lateral vignettes and by small balloons poised among the sequin-laden flowers.

The gondola with its two passengers clearly identifies the hydrogen balloon of M. Charles. The oval scene (left) may depict the hot-air type of the Montgolfier brothers. The early aeronauts gave their names to their inventions, known popularly as charlières or montgolfières. Decoration au ballon was the mark of fashion.

France, ca. 1784
Gouache on silk, gold thread and sequins
Ivory sticks; guard: 27.3 cm (10¾ in)
Gift of Mrs. Reginald Rives
Acc. no. 1978.10.16

hough ineffective for moving air, the lace fan
s everything else in its favor. The point plat
Venise, delicate-looking but sturdy, makes
exquisite leaf, set off by widely-spaced ivory
cks. A loop for a ribbon must have been add-
at the rivet about a century later.

A slightly earlier fan of needle lace was no. 109
of the Felix Tal collection exhibited at
Beeckestijn in 1979. These early lace fans
heralded a trend toward textile leaves that
gained momentum throughout the nineteenth
century. They substituted the abstract beauty of
lace for pictorial decoration.

France, 1770-85
Lace leaf
Ivory sticks; guard: 27.3 cm (10¾ in)
Gift of Archer M. Huntington
Acc. no. 16,185

"The Ladies Travelling Fan of England and Wales" was published by T. Balister for the Londoner. It shows the principal roads, rivers, market and post towns with their distances from London. The southern part of England is shown on the front, the northern part on the reverse, with a slight overlap.

This map fan is a fine example of the aid-to-memory type. Two duplicates are known: one was part of Lady Charlotte Schreiber's collection; the other, belonging to the Hamman collection, was exhibited at the British Museum in 1979. The county borders were added when the print was colored by hand.

England, Sept. 13, 1788
Hand-colored print on paper
Wooden sticks; guard: 25 cm (9¾ in)
Gift of Mrs. S. Coursing
Acc. no. 9206

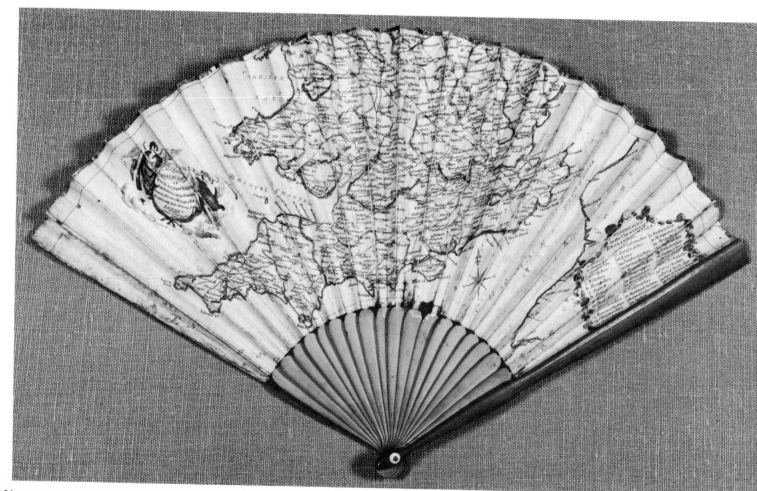

Two young people fly their tethered birds like small kites under a wide blue sky. Bird cages and captive birds are familiar eighteenth-century subjects, often charged with amorous meaning (see no. 20). Coquetry seems minimal in this scene of gentle natural beauty.

Contemporary English gardens were deliberately artless, with informal masses of "natural" planting. Long vistas sometimes ended in a fine ruin or a Greek temple. The sticks here provide the same kind of surprise. Their fine carving may show Briseis' return to the hero Achilles.

England, 1790-95
Gouache on vellum
Ivory sticks; guard: 24 cm (9½ in)
California Midwinter International Exposition
Acc. no. 3815

An oval painting enclosed in a laurel border shows two young women listening to a flute player. One holds a shepherd's crook. This pastoral scene is centered on a delicate arcade, each archway framing a pineapple. A decorated gold band borders the leaf on all sides.

A fan leaf by Angelica Kauffmann at the Victoria and Albert Museum has panels of grotesque ornament of similar elegance. Kauffmann's work is associated with Robert Adam's classical interiors. The ivory sticks, forming a Wedgwood-like cartouche, preserve that neoclassical connection.

England, ca. 1790
Gouache on vellum
Ivory sticks; guard: 26.7 cm (10½ in)
Gift of Sarah Spooner
Acc. no. 25498

FANS: 1800-1920

By 1800 fans were at the vanishing point. If the *merveilleuse* carried a fan at all, it was an "imperceptible." As a rule, her hands were quite full enough with veil, train, reticule, and the predictable Kashmir shawl clutched over her muslin chilliness. The belle of the next generation was less active. Laced into semi-immobility and much given to dreaming and sighing, she retrieved from time's dustbin that most romantic of all accessories. The small horn brisé fans, sometimes called "minuet" fans, were innovations of her day. Her rediscovery of the fans of the *ancien régime* had more lasting consequences.

These fans came to public attention during an exercise in nostalgia — in itself an evidence of romanticism. The Duchesse de Berry organized a ball at the Tuileries in 1827. She planned four quadrilles, the third to be in the style of Louis XV. A search for old court fans to serve as props for the event led to the shop of Vanier, rue Caumartin, who had made such a collection. The fans created a sensation, followed by an immediate market for antique fans. Agents searched for old fans abroad, where emigrés fleeing the Terror had left fans as souvenirs in the foreign homes that had given them shelter. The fan maker Desrochers found the hunting particularly good in Holland. Many other fans were repatriated from England, Belgium, and Germany.

The demand, however, outdistanced the supply and soon fan makers had a new serious business of copying old fans. The Gimbel brothers of Strasbourg were among the most successful between the years 1846-51. The fidelity of the copies depended on the intention of the fan maker as well as his skill. Some hoped to pass off their fans as originals; others aimed only at recapturing the eighteenth-century spirit. *The Elopement of Helen* (no. 40), for example, copies a known eighteenth-century fan. *Viva España* (no. 41), although probably a "new" design, is such a production that, like no. 40, it seems intended to deceive. The *Concert Champêtre* (no. 43) is a much less elaborate fan. Perhaps for this reason, it looks like a neo-rococo confection, made with no serious pretense of authenticity. Descending the scale, the well-painted no. 44 is merely retrospective and no. 45 has the historical ambition of a Valentine.

Inevitably, the old themes were recycled along with the form and the manner. Cathay proved as durable as the Trojan War and the amorous shepherds. Nos. 38 and 39, both made for export, show respectively two sages in contemplation and the gentle delights of a Cantonese garden. The last reprise of the eighteenth-century theme (no. 69) was too faint to be heard.

The fans of the Janus-like nineteenth century faced forward about 1870. Perhaps the Franco-Prussian War had dealt romanticism a fatal blow. Pictorial subjects were outdated. Fans began to be seen as part of the whole ensemble, telling us less about people's thoughts and more about their costumes. We see the heavy silks and satins of the House of Worth in nos. 50-53, the laces from Belgium and France that Victorian ladies knew, loved and added to their dresses (nos. 54, 55, 58), and feathers in increasing amounts. Imported feathers from distant lands and the barnyard variety dyed to look exotic appeared on fans as they had on hats, muffs, and even an occasional dress (nos. 49, 59, 60). The whole stuffed bird found on bonnets of the mid-eighties also "graced" fans of that and earlier periods (no. 48). The majestic proportions of the 1890s demanded outsized birds (nos. 66, 67).

The fan acquired new roles in the early twentieth century. Fans with pictorial representation appeared, generally with an axe to grind — some advertising (nos. 65, 72), others propagandizing (no. 73). The most elegant are the personal ornaments of a privileged class (nos. 62, 74, 75). The last fans in the collection have a dynamic role in which fan and fanner blend. The undulating petals, the swaying plumes of nos. 71 and 76 are only as expressive as the hand that holds them.

France, ca. 1810

England, 1820-30

China, ca. 1860

SPANGLED FEATHERS

France, ca. 1880

U.S.A., ca. 1870

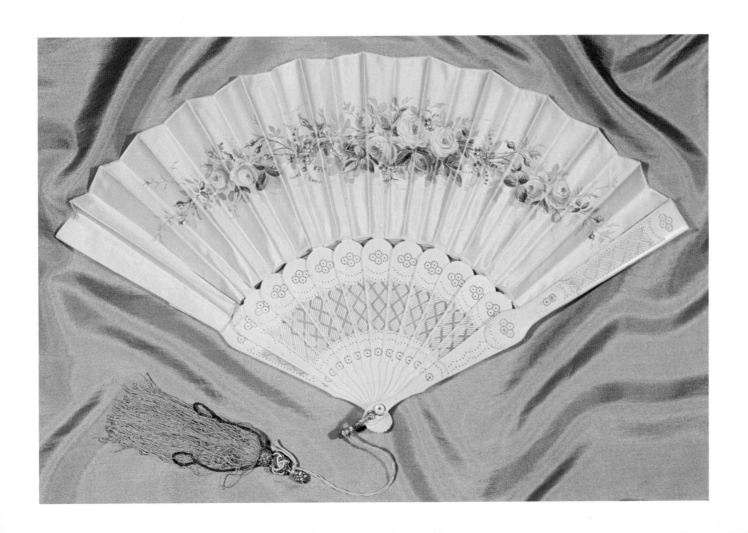

DANTE'S DREAM

England or France, after 1881

Germany, 1892

France, 1915

The English potter Josiah Wedgwood caught the neo-classic spirit by placing cool, white friezes on the deep tones of his stoneware. The seven amorini in grisaille set against a blue field recall Wedgwood's scheme. They pursue the graphic and plastic arts and the sciences of geography and astronomy.

A single cupid decorates each guard. Short inner sticks of blue and white alternate with sticks carrying animal cameos. The fan's small size and white silk leaf, brilliant with sequins, was designed to complement the First Empire styles of the turn of the century.

England, ca. 1800
Sequins and gouache on silk
Ivory sticks; guard: 24 cm (9½ in)
Gift of Mrs. Reginald Rives
Acc. no. 1978.10.6

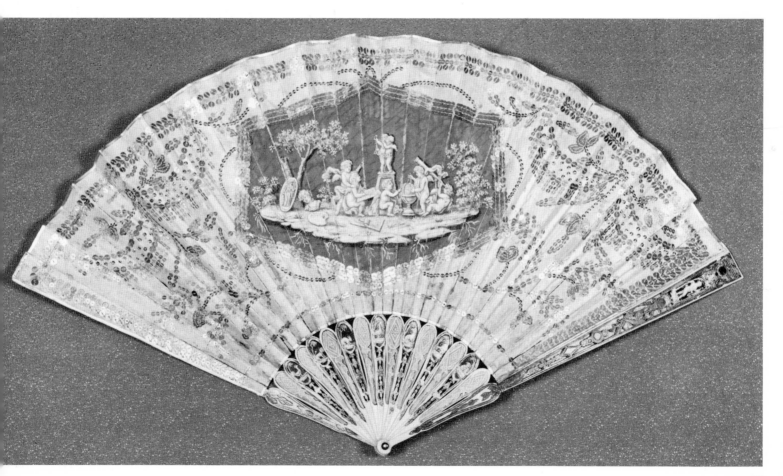

The formal symmetry of the white silk leaf encrusted with sequins recalls the fashions of the First Empire. Satin-stitch embroidery in brilliant colors and fringed garlands of laid gold thread enrich the design of stylized flowers.

The fringed garlands appear again in gold and silver leaf on the short sticks, together with three cartouches enclosing hunting motifs and musical instruments. A bird and dog are silhouetted on the guard against coppery foil. The rivet is inset with green paste.

France, ca. 1810
Silk, gold and colored threads, sequins
Bone sticks; guard: 24 cm (9½ in)
Gift of Mrs. Reginald Rives
Acc. no. 1978.10.11

Nationalist and religious sentiment spurred the Gothic revival of the early nineteenth century. Neo-Gothic churches sprang up everywhere, and Gothic ruins became tourist meccas. This small brisé fan has crocket endings, gilt window tracery, painted statues in niches, and views of a stately ruined church.

The ruins are set in an open countryside. Small figures climb stairs leading nowhere or gaze at vine-draped arches against a blue sky. Some specific site may be depicted, like the splendid ruins of Rievaulx Abbey in northern Yorkshire, and the fan may have been intended as a souvenir.

England, 1820-30
Paint and gilt on horn
Guard: 18.5 cm (7¼ in)
Gift of Mrs. Morton Mitchell
Acc. no. 44659

Two swan-necked gondolas filled with revelers glide under a full moon to the sound of music. The diners at center drink a toast; a group at right fishes by torchlight. The romantic scene is framed by a hand-painted gold border.

An eighteenth-century wedding procession is depicted on the reverse. The bride sits on a donkey. She and her entourage are led by musicians and a bottle-waving rustic. The crudely carved sticks, overlaid with gold foil, were probably made in the Philippines.

Spain, ca. 1835; signed Eug. Andre Paper; hand-colored lithograph, gilded Mother-of-pearl sticks; guard: 24 cm (9½ in) Gift of Estate of Charlotte C. Elsasser Acc. no. 56.27.2

On the face of this mourning fan an elaborately coiffed young woman is carried heavenward by two angels. Three women mourn at right, and a disconsolate mourner in doublet and hose weeps at left. The fan is painted in gray and black with touches of silver.

The couple in happier days is depicted on the reverse. She reads as her lover listens. Banners beside the arch are inscribed "O. Rouan" and "Ce-Gay." Pictorial mourning fans were used until the mid-nineteenth century (see no. 18).

Spain, ca. 1830
Hand-colored print on paper
Mother-of-pearl sticks; guard: 28.5 cm (11 1/4 in)
Gift of Estate of Charlotte C. Elsasser
Acc. no. 56.27.3

Masqueraders celebrate a carnival in a park-like setting with a palm tree. Some dance; others merely watch or play the clown. The men, for the most part, wear or carry grotesque, full-face masks. The unmasked women wear the coiffures and dresses of their day, shortened to theater length and sufficiently modified to qualify as costumes.

The subject on the reverse is unrelated to the carnival. Six women cluster around a letter-writer on a cloud-borne pavilion. Stenciled designs fill in the corners and band the top. The Fine Arts Museums' collection includes another Spanish carnival fan and a fan that is itself a mask (no. 10).

Spain, ca. 1835
Hand-colored print on paper
Wooden sticks; guard: 30 cm (11¾ in)
California Midwinter International Exposition
Acc. no. 3810

Men, women, and children in contemporary dress stroll by the water's edge. The lithographed scene has a decorative border similar to those of nos. 34 and 35. The classical scene on the reverse probably represents Venus and Adonis with his hunting dogs.

Back and front are divided into the same broad color areas of blue, brown, and pink, probably laid in with broad strokes by a brush-boy. The inner bone sticks are painted and gilded; the guards are mother-of-pearl. Some fans with round holes were fitted with lenses.

Spain, ca. 1840
Hand-colored lithograph on paper
Bone and mother-of-pearl sticks;
guard: 21.5 cm (8½ in)
Anonymous gift
Acc. no. X1980.12

The theme of two scholars in conversation appears often in Ming and Ch'ing painting. The bamboo at left symbolizes the man of character who bends in the wind but does not break. The spareness of design is typically Chinese, as is the classic cloud behind the moon. The scholar's features seem European.

The brisé blades are made of pliable metal threads soldered together. The design has been executed in the cloisonné technique (the vitreous glaze is fused to the metal within partitions called cloisons that define outlines and details). The fan is purely decorative, as ineffective in use as a sieve.

China for export, ca. 1860
Enamel on silver filigree
Guard: 19 cm (7½ in)
Gift of Estate of Charlotte C. Elsasser
Acc. no. 56.27.16

A delicate leaf of Brussels bobbin and needle lace surmounts extraordinary ivory sticks carved in China for European export. The rounded shoulder of the guard stick is formed by the head and wings of a bat, an oriental symbol for good luck. The inner sticks depict activities in a Cantonese garden.

Here smiling figures pursue their peaceful pleasures among large-scale flowers and small-scale trees. Some watch from gazebos. Others fan, meditate, catch birds and butterflies, or go boating. The garden in mirror image is carved on the reverse.

Netherlands (leaf), China (sticks), ca. 1865
Ivory sticks; guard: 26 cm (10¼ in)
California Midwinter International Exposition
Acc. no. 3802

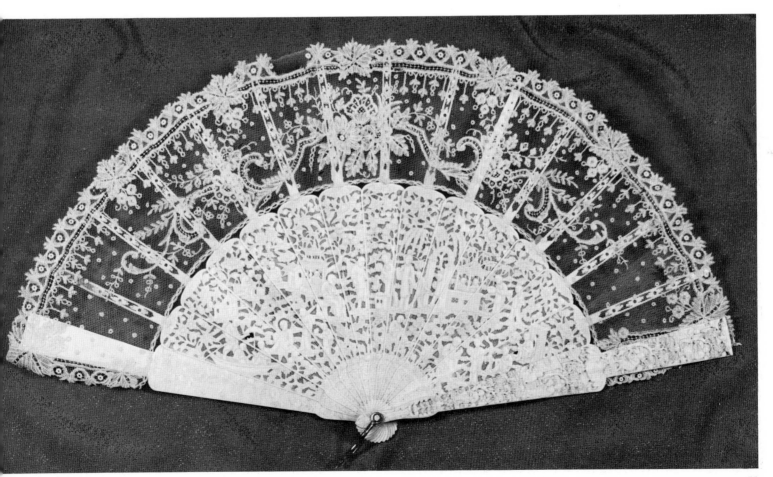

The artist based his design on an eighteenth-century model, reducing the number of figures by half and giving them sweeter expressions. The event that precipitated the Trojan War moves the principals to sentiment rather than passion. The scene was transferred to a wider leaf and surrounded with putti, fruit, and flowers.

The heavily ornate sticks contrast with those of the original. They are intricately pierced and extravagantly gilded. Sheets of iridescent mother-of-pearl (possibly tinted) were laid behind the groups of gold-leaf figures. No expense was spared in this attempt to create a luxurious fan in the eighteenth-century manner.

France, second half 19th century
Lithograph on paper
Mother-of-pearl sticks; guard: 30.5 cm (12 in)
Gift of Mrs. Reginald Rives
Acc. no. 1978.10.14

The centrally located coat of arms has not been identified, although most of its elements are well known. The trimmed branches (lower right) are, perhaps, explained by the narrative scene of the leaf in which Spaniards, armed only with such branches, try to prevent Turkish archers from abducting their women.

A Spanish-Turkish naval engagement takes place on the reverse under a banner inscribed Viva España. A nineteenth-century date is suspected because of the style of the putto, the costumes after Cesare Vecellio on the obverse, the presence of an occasional mid-nineteenth-century hairstyle, and the handsome but latter-day sticks.

Spain, 19th century
Gouache on vellum
Mother-of-pearl sticks; guard: 30.5 cm (12 in)
Gift of Mrs. B. Greenough
Acc. no. 1964.94

Fans with biblical subjects were suitable for church. David, bent on vengeance, was met by Abigail with asses bearing bread, wine, corn, sheep, and fruit. I Samuel 25 tells how she softened David's anger and later became his wife. The reverse has a landscape in the style of Claude Lorrain.

The color and painting do not seem inconsistent with an eighteenth-century date, but the sticks raise serious doubts. Old ivory sticks have been fitted with mother-of-pearl panels, extended by some sort of transparent material. The guards are a pastiche of bits and pieces, the joins disguised by crude flower garlands.

Italy, 18th century on later sticks
Gouache on vellum
Ivory, mother-of-pearl sticks;
guard: 26 cm (10¼ in)
Gift of Mrs. Reginald Rives
Acc. no. 1978.10.9

Unique in the Museums' collection, the mechanical fan defies classification. It has the handle of the rigid fan (no. 46), but a folding leaf. Its resemblance to the Cockade (no. 56) is modified by its ingenious gadgetry. The pleated satin leaf can be retracted into its case by drawing the knob toward the handle.

In use, the knob is pushed to the end of the slot, given a turn, and the fully extended leaf spins slowly by clockwork. Two kinds of mother-of-pearl were combined in the handle and case. The gold lip Pinctada maxima *was used for the handle, the black lip* Pinctada margaritifera *for the case.*

U.S.A. or France, 1870-80
Satin leaf
Mother-of-pearl handle-case; 16 cm (6¼ in)
California Midwinter International Exposition
Acc. no. 3834

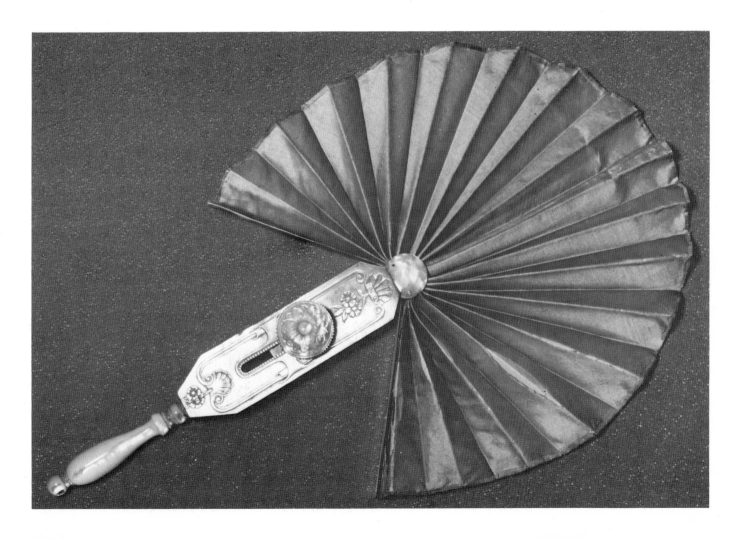

Rigid fans had been used for millenia before the invention of the folding fan. This example is Canadian, perhaps made by Indians. It copies a Brazilian wedding fan sometimes called the "Valentine" fan, of which many examples have been published. Most of these have humming-birds attached to the leaf.

The center of the leaf is probably white egret, dyed bright pink at the edges. An entire stuffed yellow warbler is fixed at the center in an attitude of flight. Morning glories are embroidered on the handle in quill or vegetable fiber. The back is supported by strong white goose feathers.

Canada, ca. 1860
Egret feathers, yellow warbler
Birchbark handle; 11.5 cm (4½ in)
Gift of Lucy S. Brewer
Acc. no. 853R

The feathers of this small green fan and their place of assemblage are both controversial. Pheasant feathers are identified by their distinctive marking. They were dyed deep green (now faded) and given a lustrous edging taken from the peafowl (Pavo cristatus).

Fan experts believe the feathers may have been exported from Malaysia. The spangles seem to be a European addition. Inexpensive copies of this kind of fan were made with "feathers" of paper. The singer Jenny Lind is said to have introduced a type with silk cut out in the shape of feathers.

France, ca. 1880
Peafowl and pheasant feathers
Tortoiseshell sticks; guard: 11.5 cm (4½ in)
Gift of Mrs. George Bowles
Acc. no. 54836

The ivory brisé fan popular in the 1830s inspired this example. It was realized with new fussiness. The carving was probably done after 1859 by a mechanical device whose work "rivaled the products of China." The Philippines may be the place of manufacture, but the satin was almost certainly added in Europe.

A brisé fan incorporating a textile seems a contradiction. Here thin vertical strips of satin have been applied individually to each brisé blade to give the illusion of a continuous leaf. The elaboration adapts an old style to the heavily ornate fashions of the 1870s.

Philippines, ca. 1870
Ivory with satin
Guard: 20.5 cm (8 in)
Gift of Virginia Kornfeld
Acc. no. 26591

The satin leaf is carefully painted with a long spray of cabbage roses and forget-me-nots, both with well-known meanings in the language of flowers. The slightly off-center position of the spray suggests a loss on the right hand, a supposition supported by the mended guard.

The fan was probably made in one of America's early fan factories. The oldest, started by Edmund S. Hunt, began to prosper in 1870-71, when the Franco-Prussian War curtailed French imports. Hunt's memoirs mention a carving machine. The fan has a Spanish silk tassel.

U.S.A., ca. 1870
Paint on satin
Ivory sticks; guard: 24 cm (9½ in)
Gift of E. Sussman
Acc. no. 40.8.8

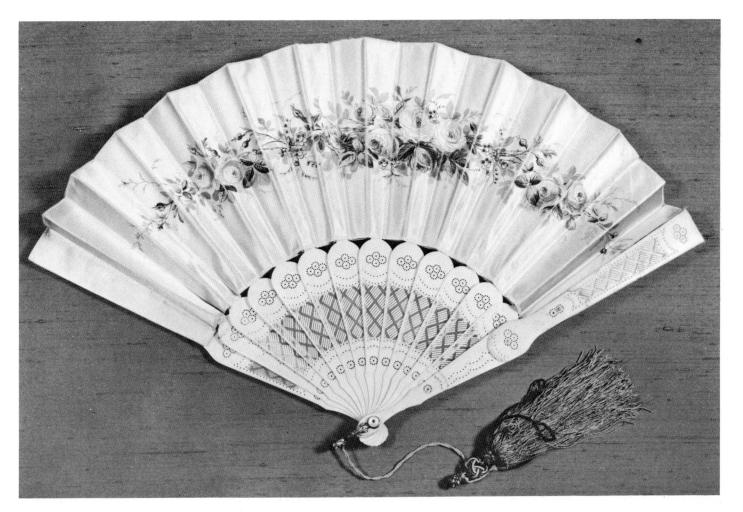

ASYMMETRICAL FAN

This fan's decorative impact comes from its asymmetrical leaf and the long curve of its sticks. The prototype was certainly Japanese, but this example of heavy satin edged with feathers may have been made in France after an oriental model. Japanese influence in the mid-seventies left its mark on all the arts.

Miss Esther Oldham's famous collection of fans included an asymmetrical one with a symbolic interpretation. A temple was carved on the guards. With the fan open, the sticks formed steps leading to the temple. The present fan probably has no such symbolic meaning. It may have been actually Japanese-made for export.

France or Japan, ca. 1880
Satin leaf with feathers
Ivory sticks; guard: 30 cm (11¾ in)
Gift of Mrs. E. Rosner
Acc. no. 36715

The monogram M.A.T. is the focal point of the bright blue moiré leaf. The letters are appliquéd in fine bobbin lace. A square-linked chain of the same lace makes three deep swags, held in place visually by floral sprays. The tinted mother-of-pearl sticks echo the blue tone of the leaf.

Throughout the eighteenth century, mother-of-pearl sticks were enhanced by encrustations of gold and silver, by painting as well as by carving and piercing. The dyeing of mother-of-pearl was a nineteenth-century invention. Worth's promotion of stiff and opulent fabrics is seen in the use of satin and moiré for fan leaves.

France, ca. 1870
Watered silk leaf
Mother-of-pearl sticks; guard: 27.3 cm (10¾ in)
Gift of Mrs. B. Greenough
Acc. no. 1964.108

The Victorian age was not afraid of color. Delicate black lace contrasts boldly with sticks dyed a brilliant yellow. Cupid aims an arrow in the central medallion, flanked by Empress Eugenie's favorite field flowers. Extra width at the right edge prevents the guard from spoiling the design's symmetry.

Chantilly lace was named for the French town where it was first made. Later Grammont, Belgium, and Bayeux, France, were known for Chantilly, furnishing not only fan leaves, but parasol covers, mantillas, and other luxury items. This finished fan came from Rodien, Paris. Its magenta velvet fan box survives.

France, ca. 1870
Lace leaf
Mother-of-pearl sticks; guard: 28 cm (11 in)
Gift of Barbara D. Jostes
Acc. no. 78.56.17

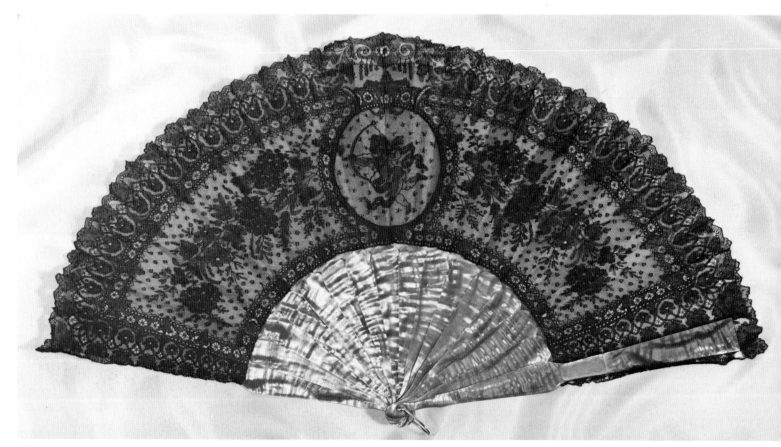

The rose point leaf makes an interesting comparison with Brussels Lace, no. 58. Here the lace is coarser; the rose petals have fewer layers. The asymmetrical placement of the lace design has lessened its formality. This small fan may have been intended for a young girl.

The sticks and the ribs are made in one piece of "reconstituted amber" (see no. 74). The material, presumed to be some kind of resin, has been moulded or pressed into a rinceau design at the top of the guards. A loop of the same material once held a ribbon.

France, 1890-1900
Lace leaf
Plastic sticks; guard: 18cm (7in)
Gift of Mrs. Charles Shainwald
Acc. no. 55045

Centuries before folding fans were imported to Europe from the Orient, a fan with circular folding leaf was used in Christian ritual. The old Roman flabellum was its model; its main purpose was to keep flies from the Host during the mass. This pleated silk fan is a late interpretation of that ancient type.

The silk is attached to wooden handles covered with black velvet. Fully extended, the leaf opens 360° to form a cockade. It can be released and folded back to lie flat between the sticks. Entirely without color, it may have been intended for a man's use.

Origin unknown, 1850-70
Black silk, wooden handles; guard: 25.4 cm (10 in
Anonymous gift
Acc. no. S353

This ivory brisé fan belonged to Dr. Carl von Hoffman (1858-1917) and was given in his memory. The initials CVH under a baron's coronet are carved on the guard and incised on the medallion provided for belt attachment. The fan was probably made in the Orient for export to Germany.

A clip on the medallion's reverse and a chain of square ivory links ending in a hook allow the fan to be suspended from the belt. The long spray of forget-me-nots and the crowned monogram on the guard are both carved in very high relief.

China or Japan for export, ca. 1890
Ivory blades; guard: 21 cm (8¼ in)
Gift of Mrs. G.T. Otten
Acc. no. 54.53.13

The leaf is entirely of needlepoint lace, except for the small bobbin lace rosettes at the edges. Eight roses with three-dimensional petals are spaced over the leaf with an oval of smaller roses in the center. The design's symmetry contributes to its formality.

The ground of point de gaze is made of a single thread and so fine that the design seems to float above the pierced mother-of-pearl ribs. The rose motif, characteristic of Brussels, was particularly popular late in the century and was often associated with weddings.

Brussels, 1870-80
Lace leaf
Mother-of-pearl sticks; guard: 28.5 cm (11¼ in)
Gift of Barbara D. Jostes
Acc. no. 78.56.5

A frankly frivolous subject is presented with ambivalence. Is the cat mewing pitifully with eyes closed, or stealing a sly side-long glance? A. Thomasse painted this conversation piece with humor and his cat's meow announces a new spirit in fan design.

The stick construction, identical to no. 62, is more discernible in the lighter material. The back of the leaf is signed by Duvelleroy, whose house, established about 1800, is still in business. A border of gold sequins accents the rippling edge, giving a shell-like finish.

France, ca. 1905
Paint on silk
Simulated horn; guard: 14 cm (5½ in)
Gift of Mrs. Donald Frothingham
Acc. no. 52.23.5

The centuries-old custom of collecting the signatures of one's friends gained widest acceptance in the nineteenth century. The ubiquitous autograph album was joined by the autograph fan with leaves left blank for names and sketches or with brisé blades prepared for that purpose.

A group of Munich art students signed and painted this wooden fan in 1892. Some used a single blade; others covered two or three with contrasting images and varying degrees of skill. Their collective project is a sampler of their interests and their taste.

Germany, 1892
Oil paint on wood
Guard: 32 cm (12½ in)
Anonymous gift
Acc. no. X1980.1

his souvenir from the World's Columbian Ex-
osition shows the rounded dome of the palace
 Agriculture (right) and the long arcades of the
Manufacture and Liberal Arts buildings (left).
 visitor standing before the Administration
uilding and looking across the Grand Basin
ould have had this view.

The allegorical figure, possibly intended to
represent the Republic, differs from the statue
still standing in Jackson Park. She has been
given a spindly throne and an entourage of
cherubs holding symbols of Industry, Art, and
Science. Prominent among the flowers in the
corners are goldenrod, lilac, and pansies.

U. S. A. (Chicago), 1893
Lithograph on paper
Wooden sticks; guard: 34 cm (13 ½ in)
Gift of M.H. de Young (?)
Acc. no. X1980.6

This stately fan with a spread of 74 cm (29 in) is made of twenty brown and white ostrich plumes. These are mounted on 13-cm (5-in) tortoiseshell sticks held together by a brown ribbon. The tortoiseshell ring attached at the rivet end holds a silk cord and tassel.

Ostrich fans were numerous at this period, but this example has an unusual feature. A watch with gold hands and Roman numerals is mounted in the guard. Armstrong illustrates a similar fan, without a watch but equipped with a jeweled guard, that she attributes to Russia.

France, 1890-1900
Natural ostrich feathers
Tortoiseshell sticks; guard: 26.7 cm (10½ in)
Gift of Jerome Bachman
Acc. no. 55.22.2

...gle feathers of different lengths are mounted ...a boldly asymmetrical design. The sticks are ... early type of amber-colored plastic strung ...gether with a ribbon. The fan spans 84-cm ...3-in) when fully opened.

The number of surviving feather fans attests to their success at the turn of the century. For a time there was a strange interest in suggesting the whole bird. Entire pheasants nested on stylish hats, and stuffed birds appeared on fans. This striking fan evokes an eagle's wing outstretched in flight

France, ca. 1900
Natural eagle feathers
Plastic sticks; guard: 24cm (9½ in)
Gift of Mrs. B. Greenough
Acc.no. 1964.100

The magician's fan opened in the usual way from left to right presents a normal appearance. Its alternating bands of pink and green ribbon are finished with a double bow at the rivet. However, if the fan is opened in the other direction, the leaf disintegrates, falling into separate sections.

While the pieces dangle before the shocked onlookers, the fan can be magically restored by reopening it again from left to right. The secret of the sleight-of-hand lies in double sticks that hook together in one direction.

Japan for export, ca. 1890
Ribbon leaf
Wooden sticks; guard: 34 cm (13½ in)
Gift of Mrs. Donald Frothingham
Acc. no. 52.23.4

The pensive lady in the sedan chair is beseiged by a swarm of cupids, like the eighteenth-century marchande d'amours. *The banality of subject and expression, though delicately painted, marks a low ebb in artistic invention. It is clear that the stalled vehicle epitomizes a genre that was going nowhere.*

Six elaborate mother-of-pearl sticks, full-length like the guards, lie above the gauze leaf. The intervening short sticks connect with long, pierced ivory ribs supporting the leaf from behind. The decorative treatment of the sticks and their innovative arrangement constitute the fan's principal interest.

France, ca. 1900
Paint on gauze
Mother-of-pearl sticks; guard: 33 cm (13 in)
Gift of Barbara D. Jostes
Acc. no. 78.56.4

The leaf is thin silk gauze, the sticks carved sandalwood, probably imported from the Orient. These are traditional materials for the large fans of the 1890s. The off-center placement and intensity of color are new. The painting, signed Dailliard, has a sketch's informality.

Buds and full-blown roses are crushed together at the left side. The right side is underfurnished with only sparse foliage and a large moth that has alighted at the edge. The sticks are stamped with gold, and gold threads enrich the soft green silk tassel.

France or England, ca. 1900
Paint on gauze
Wooden sticks; guard: 29 cm (11½ in)
Gift of Barbara D. Jostes
Acc. no. 78.56.9

This imaginative fan is a study in motion. Its twenty-one chiffon "petals" are attached individually to each of the ribs, their rounded tops and free edges weighted with small metal clips. As the fan is carried, its delicate flanges move expressively with an undulating, submarine grace.

The connection is close between this fan and the gentle clothes that preceded World War I. It also hints at fashions to come — the heavily beaded dresses of the twenties, for example, that were designed to be worn and seen in constant motion. The painted sticks, like the petals, have finely serrated edges.

France, ca. 1915
Chiffon with metal clips
Wooden sticks; guard: 35 cm (13¾ in)
Gift of Barbara D. Jostes
Acc. no. 78.56.3

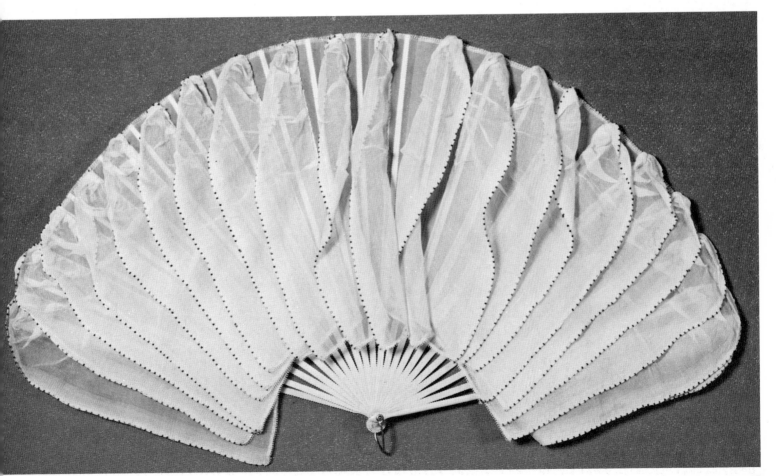

About the time of World War I, fans began to advertise cafés, perfumes, liquor, and more useful products like the sewing machine. On the leaf of the mass-produced Singer fan an abstract form of the machine's sewing arm embraces three groups of hand-painted flowers. Sticks and guards are stamped.

A sewing machine was invented in 1830, but its chain stitch had the disadvantage of unraveling at a moment's notice. Isaac Singer improved on Elias Howe's lockstitch model and patented his invention in 1851. The Singer advertising fan was given away at the Panama Pacific Exposition of 1915 in San Francisco.

Japan for export to U.S.A., 1915
Handcolored print on paper
Wooden sticks; guard: 21.5 cm (8½ in)
Gift of Miss Amy Edwards
Acc. no. 78.68.10

A cock crows at sunrise above the flags of France and her allies, commemorating French defiance and courage in the early years of World War I. Cannon menace the peaceful valley of steeples and steep-roofed houses. The stork nesting on the roof peak specifies the province of Alsace.

The Romans used the word *gallus* to mean both "cock" and "Gaul." The bird symbolized bravery and vigilance. Its association with St. Peter added the idea of a call to duty. War-torn Alsace, lying between Germany and France, showed the indomitable spirit of France as it waited for the sun of liberation.

France, 1915
Gouache on wood
Guard: 16 cm (6¼ in)
Gift of Mrs. B. Greenough
Acc. no. 1964.82

La libellule, *or the dragonfly, was an accepted French symbol of happiness. Perhaps its erratic, zig-zag flight above the water suggested a course of carefree pleasure. The dragonflies of the fan have sequin bodies. Random sequins glitter on the painted yarrow blossoms and waterlilies.*

The shape of the gauze leaf foretells Art Deco. The composition of the sticks has not been chemically determined. They may have been made from some kind of pressed resin, known to dealers as "reconstituted amber." The sticks are decorated with silver piqué and gold paint. Bone ribs support the leaf.

France, ca. 1920
Paint and sequins on gauze
Simulated amber sticks; guard: 16.5 cm (6½ in)
Gift of Barbara D. Jostes
Acc. no. 78.56.18

In the old language of flowers that gave each variety symbolic meaning, pansies stood for thoughts, from their French name pensées. The pansies decorating this folding fan are thin slices of mother-of-pearl attached to the gauze leaf with an outline of sequins.

Sequins also define the leaves of white silk and the scrolling stems. The sticks are enriched with silver piqué. The fan's shape and the design of the sticks anticipate Art Deco. When not in use, the fan hung from the arm by a ribbon attached to the silver loop.

France, ca. 1920
Gauze with mother-of-pearl and sequins
Mother-of-pearl sticks; guard: 16 cm (6 ¼ in)
Gift of Jane Scribner
Acc. no. 49.10.39

Ostrich fans were nothing new. Splendid heavy fans with a spread exceeding 60-cm (24-in) had been carried in the nineties (no. 66). The new version reduced the number of plumes to five, three or even one and dyed them brilliant colors. A shade of orange called "Tango" was particularly popular.

It had, in fact, become inconvenient to carry a fan. The ostrich fan of the twenties was strictly a prop, designed to dramatize an evening dress with an extravagant touch of fantasy. The twentieth-century ostrich fan was closer to the Renaissance than to the Age of Victoria.

France or U.S.A., ca. 1920
Ostrich feathers
Plastic sticks; guard: 25 cm (9¾ in)
Gift of Mrs. Robert Homans
Acc. no. 1979.59.1

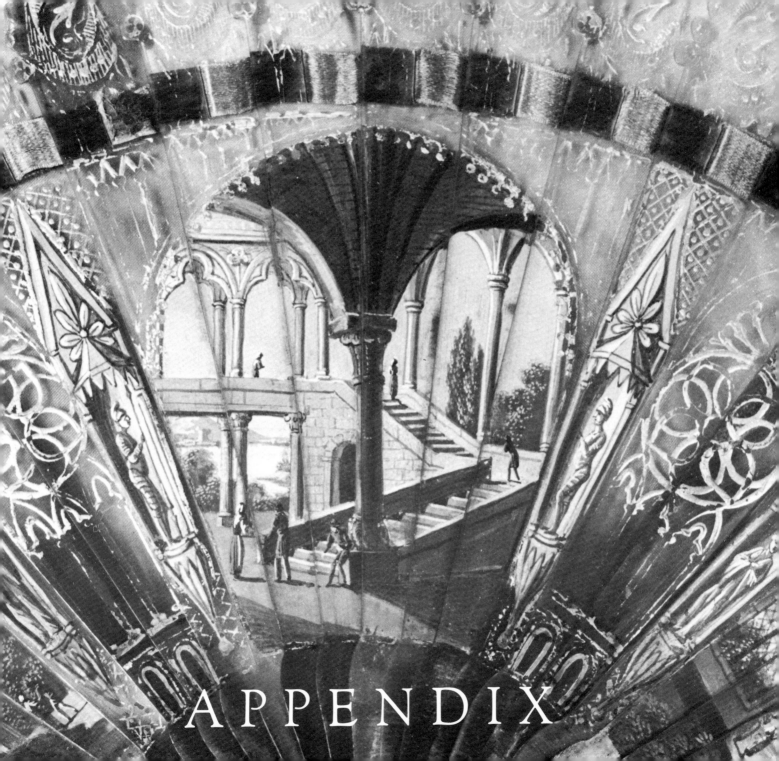

APPENDIX

1 *Abduction of Helen.* Helen and her abductor appear identically on another Louis XV fan (Percival, Pl. XX) and reversed on still another (Karlsruhe, Pl. 45). The five portraits may indicate that the fan was commissioned for a wedding, although birds on fans were considered bad luck, foretelling "quarrels and trouble" (Standen, p. 249). The composition owes something to Pietro da Cortona's *Rape of the Sabine Women* in the Capitoline Gallery.

2 *The Noble Wedding.* The ungilded sticks are carved with pastoral figures, musical putti, and rocaille ornament. Above, bunches of grapes, garlanded columns, flowers, and shells frame the wedding scene. On the reverse three figures retreat to a small island with a ruined column. The man's long waistcoat and the flowing sacque confirm the early date.

3 *Fête au Jardin.* Fans spreading to a full half circle (called *à grand vol*) became popular with the wide skirts of the 1730s-40s.

4 *Iphigenia at Aulis.* Since the fan painter did not adapt the easel painting format to his curved field, foreground details were lost when the leaf was cut to fit the sticks. The leaf has been mended and may have been mounted on later sticks.

5 *Shepherd and Shepherdess.* The costume of the figure on the guards confirms a date ca. 1765 for the sticks. On the reverse, the woman fishing remains after her companions have departed. A red paste brilliant decorates the rivet.

6 *Country Wedding.* On the reverse, a man serenades two women before an overgrown ruin while a dog drinks at the water's edge. A musette lies discarded before them. Thin mother-of-pearl sheets back the openwork of the carved sticks.

Note: Illustrations include reverses of fans or related materials where relevant.

7 *The Dispute.* Fan leaves painted with single scenes were in vogue during the first half of the eighteenth century. Here, gilt rocaille borders surround fabric-like cartouches, perhaps foretelling a new multi-scene fashion. The rivet has a paste inset.

8 *Pensent-ils au raisin?* The title is that of Boucher's painting (1747), now at the Nationalmuseum, Stockholm. The Fine Arts Museums of San Francisco have a copy (Acc. no. 72.15; see illus. above). The fan's chinoiserie reverse betrays its European origin by the woman's dress and hat and by the pots at right. The single leaf was painted before mounting, necessitating a retouching of the ribs.

9 *Mother and Children.* The scholar, in an appropriate Manchu headdress, is seated on a K'ang bed. The Chinese convention for painting rocks is also attempted. On the obverse, pairs of alternating sticks are painted to imitate blue-green stones.

10 *The Mask.* Other mask fans are in the Museum of Fine Arts, Boston (1976.176, Oldham Collection; see illus. above), The Metropolitan Museum of Art (63.90.10, gift of Mrs. William Randolph Hearst), the Armoury at the Kremlin (Armstrong, *Bulletin of the Fan Circle International,* Summer 1980, no. 15, p. 15), and in private collections in London and Paris. A sixth, from the Baldwin Collection, was auctioned at Christie's in London, May 4, 1978. Spanish newspapers, ladies in mantillas, guitars, and castanets appear in various combinations on the Boston, New York, and Christie's versions. This suggests an English manufacturer supplying fans for export to Spain as well as for home use.

11 *Bacchus and Ariadne.* Guido Reni's painting of the late 1630s, commissioned for the queen of England by Cardinal Barberini, was lost before 1640. Numerous copies had been made with compositional differences that suggest two originals. The present fan leaf and one at the Victoria and Albert Museum (Armstrong, 1974, p. 28) are closest to the copy now at the Palazzo di Montecitorio. Two other fans like the present one were noted in 1920 (Rhead, p. 122).

12 *Peasants Dancing.* A similar scene of peasants dancing appears on an engraved fan from Florence (Armstrong, 1974, pp. 34-5). A fan owned by The Metropolitan Museum of Art shows the Neopolitan lighthouse of the reverse (Standen, p. 248).

13 *Ruth and Boaz.* Boaz is shown in Middle Eastern costume, wearing loose robes and a turban. Ruth, in a fitted bodice, seems more western. The biblical scene illustrates Ruth 2:8-9.

14 *Jacob and Rachel.* The leaf illustrates Genesis 29:10. Cupid among the clouds is crudely painted on the reverse.

15 *Portraits.* The sticks, continuing the wedding theme, show an Homage to Aphrodite flanked by cupids. The leaf's intense blue surround is rather unusual. Mounted off-center, the reverse shows a couple relaxing near the water's edge.

16 *Diana and the Maidens.* While the quality of the ungilded sticks suggests they were carved in China, the use of medallions indicates they were made for export after European examples.

17 *The Abduction of Europa.* Canton porcelain export ware inspired the chinoiserie details of the reverse: pavilions with flying eaves, willows, Ming gourds, Chinese figures, and bridges. A similar brise fan with ribbon-like borders and interlocking cartouches was part of the G.J. Rosenberg collection (Rosenberg, Pl. 45).

18 *Mourning Fan.* Monuments appear frequently in eighteenth-century scenes of love (see no. 3 reverse, no. 7 obverse, no. 15 reverse). Special mourning fans were still used in the nineteenth century (see no. 35).

19 *Country Dance.* In the landscape on the reverse, a woman offers a tray to a shepherd. Laid lines are clearly visible in the handmade paper.

20 *Fête Galante.* A date in the 1770s is confirmed by heavy guards and the portraits painted in oil on ivory. A single figure and her dog inhabit the landscape on the reverse.

21 *Calendar Fan.* The holy days given chronologically are Septuagesima, Ash Wednesday, Rogation, Ascension, Pentecost, Trinity, Fête Dieu and First Sunday of Advent. Below, the dates marked "Tenis" are fast days. Solar cycle 18 (right of "1773") caused Easter to fall on April 11. The building on the reverse is crudely painted in gouache.

22 *Wallpaper Fan.* A fan leaf required a single standard sheet, approximately 30×40cm (12×16in). Oldham, (*Hobbies*, no. 3) illustrates a "domino" fan with similar roses and vertical bands.

23 *Chinese Smoker.* The Louis XV fashion for inexpensive paper fans affected even the aristocracy (Rhead, p.165).

24 *Offering to Hymen.* Aristophanes said that to gather roses and wear them in a crown was a sign of being in love (Joret, p.65). The feathers on the sticks are barred wing-coverts from the Eurasian jay (*Garrulus glandarius*).

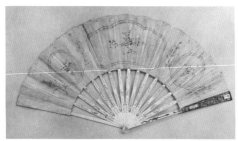

25 *Classical Wedding.* A pair of birds glides beneath rose garlands on the reverse. Carved sticks with applied gold leaf are backed by iridescent mother-of-pearl. There, musical trophies alternate between putti and pastoral figures. A fan with a similarly divided leaf and sticks *au ballon* confirms the late eighteenth-century date (Rosenberg, Pl. 58).

26 *Balloon Ascension.* Armstrong describes and illustrates the balloon fan twice (1974, p. 118, Pl. 80; 1978, pp. 32-3). In 1784-5, Clodion won the competition for a monument to be erected in the Tuileries commemorating the Charles and Robert ascension. Although the project was not realized, a terracotta model at the Louvre survives.

27 *Point de Venise.* Narrow widely-spaced sticks and guards with heavy tops were in fashion towards the end of the eighteenth century (see no. 21). Ivory guards, carved with a single figure amid birds and flowers, are backed with mother-of-pearl.

28 *Traveling Fan.* The legend gives a list of the counties in England and Wales. At least one geographical name has changed since the fan's publication in 1788: the North Sea was known as the "British Ocean."

29 *The Bird Catchers.* The monogram ("R.G.") on the reverse may indicate the fan was commissioned for a wedding. The ivory sticks, similar to those of *The Flute Player* (no. 30), were slightly damaged in the 1906 San Francisco earthquake.

30 *The Flute Player.* Robert Adam (1728-92), the foremost innovator in English neo-classical architecture and interior decoration, collaborated with Kauffmann on such projects as Kenwood and Harewood Houses. The swags and garlands on the reverse recall the designs he developed from antique sources.

31 *Arts and Sciences.* Wedgwood drew inspiration for his jasperware from the antique cameo. Foreground objects symbolize the arts: the painter's palette, architect's square, and sculptor's mallet. Gold-fringed garlands decorate other contemporary fans (no. 32; see Gasc, Fig. 130).

32 *Classical Bouquet.* A dated fan commemorating the 1802 Peace of Amiens features pierced ivory sticks of identical form and similar fringe decoration (Armstrong, 1978, pp. 74-5).

33 *Gothic Ruins.* Rievaulx Abbey, the earliest Cistercian church in England, may have inspired the central scene. Heavy cast brass guards terminate at the rivet in trefoils. For similar Gothic revival fans, see Hughes (Fig. 2), Leary (no. 20), and Karlsruhe (Pl. 63, left and right). Fashion plates from Ackermann's *Repository* of the 1820s show brisé fans with dinner, ball, and court dress.

34 *Boating Party.* Gold foil backs the openwork on the pierced guards. Armstrong (1978, p. 63) illustrates another nineteenth-century Spanish fan with hand-colored lithograph leaf and Philippine sticks.

35 *Death of a Maiden.* The cypresses on the reverse are a conventional symbol of mourning. A similar fan has been attributed to England or America, ca. 1830 (Hirshorn, Figs. 5, 5a).

36 *Carnival.* Carnival (carne, "meat" + levare, "to remove") is a traditional celebration in Roman Catholic countries marking the beginning of Lent. In New Orleans, masked balls are still an important part of Mardi Gras festivities. Both thumb guards are missing from the wooden guards.

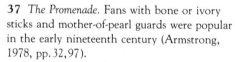

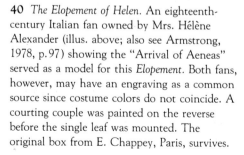

37 *The Promenade.* Fans with bone or ivory sticks and mother-of-pearl guards were popular in the early nineteenth century (Armstrong, 1978, pp. 32, 97).

38 *Silver Filigree.* Enamel colors are derived from various minerals: cobalt produces a dark lapis blue, copper a green (Rhead, p. 56). Green (Fig. 17, p. 178) and Armstrong (1978, p. 27) publish other silver filigree fans. The original ribbon has been replaced.

39 *Cantonese Garden.* A change of tone in pronouncing the Cantonese word *Fu* alters its meaning from "Bat" to "Good Luck." Many Chinese export fans of ivory and sandalwood were carved with deep undercutting. The narrow lace leaf on the top makes this one rather unusual. Armstrong has published a folding fan with similar guards (1974, pp. 154-155).

40 *The Elopement of Helen.* An eighteenth-century Italian fan owned by Mrs. Hélène Alexander (illus. above; also see Armstrong, 1978, p. 97) showing the "Arrival of Aeneas" served as a model for this *Elopement.* Both fans, however, may have an engraving as a common source since costume colors do not coincide. A courting couple was painted on the reverse before the single leaf was mounted. The original box from E. Chappey, Paris, survives.

41 *Viva España.* The pierced mother-of-pearl sticks repeat the martial theme with gilded weapons and flags on standards. Floral swags are painted near the rivet. Vecellio illustrates a Turkish pirate (no. 390), turbanned servant (no. 391), and bowman (no. 383).

42 *Abigail and David.* The figures, particularly those of David and his men, seem derived ultimately from Raphael's *Expulsion of Heliodorus* at the Vatican. A bridge with many arches spans the river on the reverse.

43 *Concert Champêtre.* Eclectic costumes reveal the nineteenth-century taste for revivals. Rychlewska (letter to AGB, 3/19/80) dates the violinist ca. 1792 (Davenport, p. 692) and the flutist ca. 1778. She places the dancer's coiffure ca. 1763 and the dress of the seated woman somewhere between 1720-62, but she sees a hairstyle of 1840 in the medallion portrait. While portrait miniatures recall eighteenth-century fashion (see no. 15), the over-gilded and over-painted sticks are strictly nineteenth-century.

44 *Marché aux Fleurs.* The Parisian Marché aux fleurs is on l'Île de la cité between the Palais de Justice and Notre-Dame de Paris.

45 *Gardening.* Wheel-like pierced designs on the sticks recall Maltese lace and lace made at Tenerife in the Canary Islands. Openwork on the guards is backed by gold foil and mother-of-pearl. The elaborate brass loop is secured by a rivet inset with paste.

46 *Handscreen.* Pâpier-maché handscreens with lacquered designs were popular earlier in the nineteenth century (White, p. 190). The Fine Arts Museums of San Francisco own an example (56.27.15) dated ca. 1820-30. Blondel (p. 69) cites Estienne's *Dialogues du nouveau language françois.*

47 *Mechanical Fan.* The pivot point for the pale lavender leaf is at the top of the case. The mother-of-pearl is decorated with carved flowers and seashells.

48 *The Yellow Warbler.* Gostelow (Fig. 20, p. 8) illustrates a very similar fan from the Schenectady Museum, Schenectady, New York. Armstrong (1978, p. 90) publishes a Brazilian example with white and yellow feathers and stuffed hummingbird.

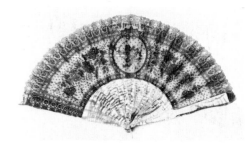

49 *Spangled Feathers.* In 1858, Adolphe Braun photographed Contessa Castiglione, favorite of Napoleon III, carrying a similar fan (Battersby, p. 236). The Fine Arts Museums of San Francisco own so-called Jenny Lind fans with "feathers" of paper (3808, 3811) and of silk (78.68.9, 1179R, 47956).

50 *Satin Brisé.* In 1859, Alphonse Baude invented machinery to cut ivory latticework which became widely used in l'Oise (Blondel, p. 297).

51 *Dance Fan.* Hunt's autobiography, *Reminiscences* (p. 151), describes the fan factory he opened with a "boiler and engine, and saws and moulders" in 1867. His early fans had machine-carved hornbeam sticks mounted with imported linen and silk. A provenance for this fan has been suggested as the factory begun by Frank Allen with Hunt's brother Fred.

52 *Asymmetrical Fan.* Asymmetry in dress trimmings and drapery was fashionable in 1875-6 (Blum, p. 77). Claude Monet's *La Japonaise* (1876) dances with an asymmetrical fan against a random arrangement of non-folding fans. China also exported fans with spiral mounts in the second half of the nineteenth century (Green, Fig. 12; Crossman, Fig. 184).

53 *Moiré and Lace.* The leafy floral border is appliquéd Brussels bobbin lace.

54 *Chantilly.* Chantilly lace is characterized by *fond simple* ground, *fond de mariage* filling, and patterns outlined with a heavy thread, called *cordonnet* (Powys, p. 31). The rivet and loop are of gold.

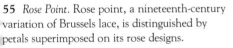

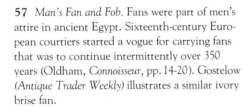

55 *Rose Point.* Rose point, a nineteenth-century variation of Brussels lace, is distinguished by petals superimposed on its rose designs.

56 *Black Cockade.* Oldham (*Connoisseur*, no. xvii), illustrates a very similar early Victorian 'British Gentleman's" cockade fan. In 1902, the Sears, Roebuck and Company catalogue offered black cockade fans of less expensive material at nine cents each (Green, p. 207).

57 *Man's Fan and Fob.* Fans were part of men's attire in ancient Egypt. Sixteenth-century European courtiers started a vogue for carrying fans that was to continue intermittently over 350 years (Oldham, *Connoisseur*, pp. 14-20). Gostelow (*Antique Trader Weekly*) illustrates a similar ivory brise fan.

58 *Brussels Lace.* The pierced mother-of-pearl sticks are incised with floral decoration.

59 *Dante's Dream.* Rosetti painted three versions of *Dante's Dream.* The second, finished in 1881 and now at the Walker Gallery, Liverpool, was the source of the obverse scene. Rosetti's model was the wife of William Morris, leading figure in the Arts and Crafts movement. The reverse scene adapts Claude's *Landscape with Samuel Anointing David King of Israel,* ca. 1643, now at the Louvre. The fan version omits all the narrative figures.

60 *Red Guinea.* Cellulose plastics began with Henri Braconnot's 1833 discovery of nitrocellulose. Work by Alexander Parkes on thermoplastics, patented in 1855, forshadowed a new industry. Sixteen years later the Celluloid Manufacturing Company was formed by John Wesley Hyatt in Albany, New York.

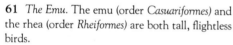

61 *The Emu.* The emu (order *Casuariformes*) and the rhea (order *Rheiformes*) are both tall, flightless birds.

62 *Silver Spangles.* In the early nineteenth century, Pierre Duvelleroy opened his fan-making establishment at 17 Passage des Panoramas, Paris. His English branch opened in 1849 at 167 Regent Street, London (Green, p. 278; Armstrong, 1974, p. 194). Another Duvelleroy fan ca. 1890 (*Berkhout*, no. 171) has a similar form.

63 *The Cat.* See note to no. 62 on Duvelleroy.

64 *Autograph Fan.* Three similar fans were in the Dreyer Collection (Rosenberg, Pl. 4). Autograph fans were made in the brisé style with wooden or ivory blades, or with folding leaves of paper or vellum. The soprano Adelina Patti had one signed by all the monarchs of Europe (Green, p. 165). Usually they held the names of personal friends (Armstrong, 1978, p. 31).

65 *Columbian Exposition Fan.* The Chicago Exposition, dedicated on October 21, 1892, commemorated the 400th anniversary of the discovery of America. Another souvenir fan in the collection, made by the Mandel Brothers, shows scenes of Columbus's landing, return to Spain, and apotheosis (illus. above).

66 *Ostrich Feathers with Watch. Harper's Bazar* showed ostrich feather fans for fashionable Victorian evening toilettes (1/2/1892, 12/23/1893; Blum pp. 236-7, 262-3). The fan illustrated by Armstrong (1978, p. 51) has undyed ostrich feathers and tortoiseshell sticks.

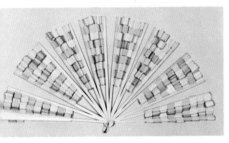

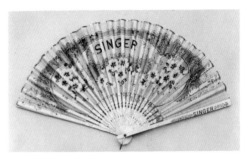

Eagle Feathers. Armstrong suggests an ustrian provenance for a similar golden eagle n (1978, p. 52). In the last decade of the nineenth century, fans tended to be either very all or outsize.

Magician's Fan. Armstrong (1978, p. 24) uses e terms "broken," "puzzle" or "trick" for fans of is type. A similar fan owned by The Fine Arts useums of San Francisco (54028) has altering cream and gold ribbons.

69 *Sedan Chair*. Fans with decorative ribs mounted on top of the leaf were "distinctly new" in 1890 (Montgomery, p. 30). *Harper's Bazar* illustrated an example the following year (9/5/1891; Blum, p. 234). *Sedan Chair* is signed at right, M. *Rodigue*.

70 *Roses*. The Fine Arts Museums of San Francisco own another gauze fan painted with roses and signed by Dailliard (78.56.6).

71 *Chiffon Petals*. The metallic clip edgings recall the Venetian glass beads that trimmed Fortuny dresses of the 1920s. Hanging from the loop, a matching pale pink ribbon survives.

72 *Singer Fan*. Modern Japanese export fans are still made with similar leaf painting and stamped guard decoration (Armstrong, 1978, p. 7).

73 *Rooster of France.* Since the Revolution, some French fans have carried political messages. The flags, left to right, represent the signers of the Proclamation of Unity: France, Great Britain, Belgium, Russia, and Italy. On the reverse, clouds cast shadows over the years 1914 and '15. Mrs. Jack Gardner's collection included a similar World War I fan (Oldham, *Spinning Wheel,* cover).

74 *Dragonflies.* Art Deco fashion favored fans with sequined gauze leaves held by pale "amber" sticks (Armstrong, 1978, p. 91). Battersby (p. 77) illustrates a similarly shaped fan dated 1921.

75 *Pansies.* The thin textile leaf with its shell and sequin ornament is entirely in accord with the decorative schemes of the 1920s when chiffon gowns were embroidered with beads, shells, or diamante. A similar fan is illustrated in Armstrong (1974, p. 161).

76 *Orange Plumes.* In 1924, the Army and Navy Co-Operative Society, Limited, of London advertised an ostrich feather fan with five plumes for 24 shillings (Green, p. 153).

Armstrong, Nancy

A Collector's History of Fans. New York: Clarkson N. Potter, 1974

The Book of Fans. New Malden: Colour Library International; New York: Mayflower Books, Inc., 1978

"Horn Fans." *Newsletter* of The Fan Circle, January 1979, pp. 12-15

Bath, Virginia Churchill

Lace. Chicago: Henry Regnery, 1974. Reprint New York: Penguin Books, 1979

Battersby, Martin

Art Deco Fashion. London: Academy Editions, 1974

Belevitch-Stankevitch, H.

Le Goût chinois en France au temps de Louis XIV. Paris: Jean Schemit, 1910

Berkhout, J.G.

Waaierweelde in Beeckestijn keuze uit het waaierkabinet Felix Tal. Exhibition catalogue. June-September 1979

Blondel, S.

Histoire des éventails chez tous les peuples et à toutes les époques. Paris: Librairie Renouard, 1875

Blum, Stella

Victorian Fashions and Costumes from Harper's Bazar 1867-1898. New York: Dover Publications, Inc., 1974

Bowie, Theodore

East-West in Art. Bloomington and London: Indiana University Press, 1966

Cavalli, Gian Carlo

Guido Reni. Florence: Vallecchi Editore, 1955

Christie's, London

Sale catalogue (Mrs. August Uihlein Pabst). Thursday, May 4, 1978 (fans)

Cornu, Paul

Galerie des Modes et Costumes Français 1778-1787. Paris: Librairie Centrale des Beaux-Arts. Reprint Paris: E. Levy, Editeur, 1911-12. 5 portfolios

Cousteau, Jacques-Yves with Philippe Diole

Life and Death in a Coral Sea. Garden City, New York: Doubleday and Co., Inc., 1971

Crossman, Carl L.

The China Trade. Princeton: Pyne Press, 1972

Davenport, Millia

The Book of Costume. New York: Crown Publishers, Inc., 1948

De Osma, Guillermo

Mariano Fortuny: His Life and Work. New York: Rizzoli International, 1980

Diderot, Denis

L'Encyclopédie, ou Dictionnaire raisonné des sciences, des arts et des métiers, Paris, 1751-65.

Didot, Amb. Firmin

Costumes anciens et modernes. Habiti antichi et moderni di tutto il mondo di Cesare Vecellio precédés d'un essai sur la gravure sur bois par M. Amb. Firmin Didot. Paris: Firmin Didot frères fils et Cie., 1859

The Fan Circle, in association with the Victoria and Albert Museum

Fans from the East. London: Debrett's Peerage Ltd. and the Victoria and Albert Museum in association with The Fan Circle, 1978

Garboli, C.

L'Opera completa de Guido Reni. Milan: Rizzoli Editore, 1971

Gasc, Nadine *et al*.

Embroidery Through The Ages. Exhibition catalogue (Museé des Arts Décoratifs, 1977). English translation, Institute for the Arts, Rice University, 1978. Exhibition at the Cooper-Hewitt Museum, New York.

stelow, Mary

e Fan. Dublin: Gill & MacMillan Ltd., 1976

een, Bertha de Vere

Collector's Guide to Fans over the Ages. London: derick Muller Ltd., 1975

vard, Henry

tionnaire de l'ameublement et de la décoration uis le XIIIᵉ siècle jusqu'à nos jours. 4 vols. Paris, 7-90

rmant, Jacques

Art à l'exposition de Chicago." Gazette des ux-Arts, September 1, 1893, pp. 237-53

rshorn, Anne Sue

ourning Fans." Antiques, April 1973

nour, Hugh

noiserie: The Vision of Cathay. London: John rray Ltd., 1961

ghes, Therle

ntasy in Plume and Parchment: European s from the Leonard Messel Collection." Coun- Life 151 (1972): 1455-58

nt, Edmund Soper

ymouth Ways and Weymouth People: niniscences by Edmund Soper Hunt. Boston: vate printing, 1907

th, Hans

quer in the West: The History of a Craft and an stry, 1550-1950. University of Chicago Press, 1

pey, Oliver

noiserie. New York: Charles Scribner's Sons, 7

nside, Robin

Raphaelite Painters. New York: Phaidon, 1948

Joret, Charles

La Rose dans l'antiquité et au moyen âge. Paris: Emile Bouillon, 1892

Lami, Stanislas

Dictionnaire de sculpteurs de l'école française au dix-huitième siècle. Paris: Honoré Champion, 1911

Leary, E.

Fans in Fashion. Exhibition catalogue. Stable Court Galleries, Temple Newsam, Leeds, 1975

Montgomery, Mary Caldwell

"Fan Histories and Fashions." The Cosmopolitan, November 1890, pp. 26-35

Oldham, Esther

"The Fan. A Gentleman's Accessory." Connoisseur 125: 14-20

"Fans of the Paper Stainers: Dominotier and Imagier." Hobbies, December 1959, pp. 28ff.

"Jenny Lind." Antiques Journal, November 1961

"Mrs. Jack's Fans." Spinning Wheel, May 1967

Powys, Marian

Lace and Lace-Making. Boston: Charles T. Branford Company, 1963

Rambo, James I.

Cathay Invoked: Chinoiserie, a Celestial Empire in the West. Exhibition catalogue. California Palace of the Legion of Honor, San Francisco, June 10-July 31, 1966

Rhead, G. Wooliscroft

History of the Fan. London: Kegan, Paul, Trubner & Co., Ltd.; Philadelphia: J.B. Lippincott, 1910

Rosenberg, Marc

Alte und Neue Facher aus der Wettbewerbong und Ausstellung zu Karlsruhe. Exhibition catalogue. Vienna: Gerlach & Schenk, 1891

Rychlewska, Maria

Letter to Anna G. Bennett. Krakow, March 9, 1980

Schreiber, Lady Charlotte

Fans and Fan Leaves. London: John Murray, 1888-90

Stalker, John and George Parker

A Treatise of Japanning and Varnishing 1688. Introduction by H.D. Molesworth. Levittown, N.Y.: Transatlantic Arts, Inc., 1972

Standen, Edith

"Instruments for Agitating the Air." Metropolitan Museum of Art Bulletin 23: 243-57

"The Story of the Emperor of China: A Beauvais Tapestry Series." Metropolitan Museum Journal, vol. 11, 1976, pp. 103-17

Tuchscherer, Jean-Michel

Etoffes merveilleuses du Museé historique des Tissus, Lyon. Japan: Gakken Co., Ltd., 1976

Vecellio, Cesare

See Didot

White, Margaret E.

"Collecting Handscreens." Antiques, April 1941, p. 190

Photography:
Jan C. Watten, Oakland, California: cover, color
plates, all Catalogue illustrations, and
nos. 27, 29, 40, and 68 in Notes to the Catalogue.
James Medley, San Francisco, California:
photographs in Notes to the Catalogue, nos. 1-7,
9, 11-26, 28, 30-39, 41-67, 69-76.
Courtesy of the Museum of Fine Arts, Boston:
no. 10 in Notes to the Catalogue.

Drawing, p. 13: Steven Sechovec.

Fans in Fashion was designed by Bruce
Montgomery, Occidental, California.
Typography, in Goudy Old Style, is by Graphic
Arts of Marin, Sausalito, California. Printed in
Japan by Dai Nippon through Interprint, San
Francisco, California